No Drama

—

NO YELLING

How to be a positive paren to grow happy child.

By Ann M. Watson

TABLE OF CONTENTS

INTRODUCTION

With each age group comes a new kind of drama, and the present parent is careful to navigate each one. Truthfully, I like yelling. Not seething, or in any event, screaming, which I informally recognize from yelling as being angrier and increasingly louder. What I'm talking about is a quick turning up the volume to transmit a message that neglected to arrive at the planned recipient in my ordinary speaking voice. Yelling is an instinctual and collective approach to express agitation. Altogether preventing parents from this mode from communicating our distress strikes me as severe and uncalled for. In this way, I will continue yelling.

As indicated by specialists, this does not make me a "bad guy". Indeed, yelling can be a weapon and a dangerous one at that. Research shows that noisy attacks can, in extraordinary circumstances, be as mentally harming as physical maltreatment. Be that as it may, yelling can be an instrument, one that lets parents discharge a little steam and, now and again, gets kids to tune in. The contrast between dangerous yelling, and typical individual getting-agitated yelling, involves substance and goal. The volume of one's voice matters, not always the communicated message.

Step by Step Instructions To Yell.

"Get your shoes on!" is, by and large, an impeccably okay thing to yell? "Try not to run in the road!" is undoubtedly OK if a child seems headed for the street. However, calling a child "ridiculous" while yelling about the shoes, or "idiotic" while yelling about the road, is beyond the reach of acceptability. Parents ought to likewise forgo addressing their children about any behavioral issues following the yell-instigating episode.

Parents let the irritation appear in our voices since we need the child to realize we are disappointed with the expectation and hope it will propel them forward. This irritation can be all right insofar as parents clarify that we are frustrated with the behavior and not merely the child. The second guideline of yelling is to think about one's crowd. Toddlers are probably not going to comprehend the substance of the yell and will ingest the disappointment, or anger. Yelling at this age is not likely going to get them to accomplish something faster or quit performing something absurd.

Focus on how a child reacts to yelling. We are altogether brought into the world with various personalities, with a few of us being unquestionably more conflict-loath than others. To confident children, a yell is only a parent being boisterous; to others, it is a specialized arraignment, and it stings.

With my children, I only need to give them a sideways look, and she knows to straighten up. Though every child is altogether different, and I expected to now and then speak loudly. Two kids in a similar family can be entirely different, and we need to change our parenting accordingly. In conclusion, mull over the recurrence with which you yell. A child who experiences childhood in a yelling-inclined family is more reluctant to ignore a solitary example of yelling than a child who experiences childhood in a calmer family.

Give kids a relentless amount of commotion during their post-toddler years, and afterward, the yelling is more likely to appear to be threatening as they grow up. Further, inoculation against the possible negative impacts of yelling originates from the way that our kids find a workable pace in life. The principles are the equivalent: We do not reprimand each other through yelling. In any case, theoretically speaking, if a parent will not get off their telephone, our first grader is allowed to speak more loudly while giving a generally harmless "please!"

Instructions To Realize The Yelling Has Gone Excessively Far.

Yelling will, in general, occur during a snapshot of elevated feelings, and increased feelings will, in general, make our judgment hazy. We may have had a valid justification to lose our cool, and however, once that cool is lost, it is anything but difficult to gain control. Parents who worry that their yelling may have veered toward rage ought to ask themselves a couple of inquiries: Was their behavior intelligible to the entire family? Were there unmistakable circumstances and logical results regarding why they get so annoyed? On the off chance that, at that point, the yelling might be damaging for the child.

The primary conclusion the child will have is that it is their fault, and they are a 'terrible' kid. However, most kids do not find a good pace, and all they know is that their parents, and the world, are unpredictable and impulsive. Almost all average, sensibly adequate parents will have harmful blasts now and again. Furthermore, as long as they are once-in-awhile, they can be helpful. I need my kids to discover that individuals do not generally carry on perfectly, and you can be in a healthy relationship where individuals lose it here and there.

This idea helps children with practicing forgiveness for other people, and parents practice forgiveness for themselves. The distinction between attempting to be a superior parent and an ideal parent is our eagerness to have sympathy for ourselves when we mess up. We can generally tell when our yelling is excessively loud or has gone on too long, given the behavior of the child. In those minutes, their response goes from receptive to observational, then attempting to understand the deeper problem, other than the socks on the ground. Children look self-protected, and their breath gets shorter. At that point, I stop. At last, they are the best manual to show us the distinction between the sort of yelling that may do hurt, and the notion that, in a noisy family like our own, it works.

CHAPTER ONE

WHY DO YOUR TODDLERS YELL?

At the point when kids get out of hand, yelling feels like a realistic reaction. Especially if parents are worried, and their resilience for hogwash has worn ragged. A parent worried over the condition of the world may yell at a child before they even acknowledge they are doing it. In any case, regardless of the way that yelling feels like a discharge, an enticement, and discipline all simultaneously, it is essential to comprehend the mental effect that yelling can have on kids. As provocative as certain behaviors may appear, little kids do not have the emotional complexity to understand grown-up disappointment completely. Also, screaming at toddlers over and over can change how their brains create and process data. A child who has been yelled at can look generally terrified or cry often. In any case, yelling at kids is profoundly unhelpful.

Yelling is a parenting "strategy" we can manage without. Luckily, there are some yelling rules to, and a few hints for helping us figure out how to quit yelling at our kids, regardless of how frustrated we may feel at the time.

Yelling at Kids Is Never Communicating.

Nobody, except a little percentage of corrupt people, appreciates being yelled at. All in all, for what reason would kids? At the point when parents yell, kids submit outwardly; however, the child is not increasingly open to your impact, they are less so. More youthful kids may bellow; more established kids will get a blank stare — yet both are shutting down as opposed to listening. That is not communication.

Adults Are Scary When They Yell at Kids.

The force parents hold over little youngsters is absolute. To them, their parents are people twice their size who give things they must have to live: Food, cover, love. At the point when the individual they trust most scares them, it shakes their conviction that all is good. Also, it is genuinely alarming for a child. They have done studies where they recorded people yelling. At the point when it was played back to the subjects, they could not accept how contorted their appearances got. A 3-year-old may seem to radiate a frame of mind like a grown-up; however, despite everything, they do not have the emotional development to be dealt with like one.

Yelling at Kids May Causes Flight or Freeze.

While parents who yell are not destroying their kids' brains, as such, they are evolving them. Suppose during a relieving experience, the brain's synapses react by conveying calming biochemicals that it is safe. That is the point at which a child is building neural pathways to quiet down.

At the point when a toddler, with the immature prefrontal cortex and no official capacity to deal with it, gets shouted at, the inverse occurs. The child discharges biochemicals that state battle, flight, or freeze. They may hit you. They may flee. Alternatively, they freeze and resemble a deer in headlights. None of those are useful for brain development. If that activity happens over and again, the behavior gets imbued.

It is Not About Letting Them Off Easy.

A parent may feel like they are putting their foot down and setting up the discipline when they yell. What they are genuinely doing is worsening the issue. Terrifying a child right now may get them to knock off what they are doing, but on the other hand, it is dissolving trust in the relationship. There is an elective technique that is progressively effective and not as stern: humor. If the parent reacts with a comical inclination, despite everything, you keep up your power. Giggling appears to be a more invited result than yelling.

Parents Who Yell at Kids Train Kids to Yell.

"Standardize" is a word that gets tossed about a great deal nowadays in governmental issues, but on the other hand, it is appropriate to a child's environment. Parents who continually yell in the house make that behavior typical for a child, and they will adjust to it. On the off chance that a child does not hesitate when an adult scolds them, there is much admonishing going on. Instead, parents need to be models of self-guideline above all else. Fundamentally, to truly get a child to carry on, adults need to first.

At the point when It is Okay to Yell at Kids.

While most of the time, yelling is not prescriptive, "there are times it is extraordinary to speak more loudly. At the point when you have kids hitting one another, similar to kin, or there is a genuine danger. These are cases while stunning those works". However, she brings up that once you stand out enough to be noticed, regulate your voice. Essentially, yell to caution, then reign it in to clarify. Nobody is going to smother themselves around their kids always, and nor should they. That is not what it means to be an individual. In any case, it is a hurtful long haul parenting technique.

The Long-Lasting Effects of Yelling at Your Kids.

In case you are a parent, you realize that occasionally feelings undo you. Some way or another, children can indeed press those buttons you did not know you had. Furthermore, before you know it, you holler from the highest point of your lungs. You are not the only one in doing that, and your sentiments of parental disappointment are typical. Fortunately, you can change how you talk to your children, changing from a yelling rant to a respectful exchange.

For what reason do parents yell?

The short answer is because we feel overpowered or furious, which makes us speak more loudly. Be that as it may, the circumstance seldom warrants that response. It might calm the children for a brief time. However, it will not make them correct their behavior or attitudes. To put it plainly, it instructs them to fear you as opposed to comprehending the outcomes of their actions.

Children depend on their parents for learning. On the off chance that anger and related animosity, like yelling, is a piece of what a child sees as "typical" in their family, their behavior will mirror that. After managing the wellbeing of your children, your primary job as a parent is to manage your feelings.

The impacts of yelling.

On the off chance that you have at any point been yelled at, you realize that a loud voice does not make the message clearer. Your children are the same. Yelling will make them block it out, and your discipline will be more intense since each time you speak more loudly, it brings down their receptivity. Yelling makes children progressively forceful, physically, and verbally. Yelling as a rule, regardless of what the specific situation, is a declaration of anger. It alarms children and causes them to feel uncertain.

Smoothness voice tones, on the other hand, is consoling, which causes children to feel loved and acknowledged disregarding disappointing behavior. On the off chance that yelling at children is anything but something to be thankful for, yelling that accompanies verbal putdowns and put-down can be qualified as emotional maltreatment. It has appeared to have long term impacts, similar to nervousness, low self-esteem, and expanded hostility. It likewise makes children progressively defenseless to harassing since their comprehension of healthy limits and self-respect are slanted.

Options in contrast to raising your voice.

Children who have a compelling emotional association with their parents are "easier" to discipline. At the point when children have a sense of security and feel genuinely cherished, they will be progressively open to talking and tune in before a conflict grows into a furious yelling scene.

Here is the way you can rehearse positive discipline that does not include yelling.

1. Give yourself a break.

Catch yourself before getting so furious that you lose control and speak loudly. By venturing ceaselessly from the conflict zone for a couple of seconds, you allow yourself to reconsider and inhale deeply, which will assist you with quieting down.

Additionally, this shows your children that you recognize your limits and gives them a healthy overseeing of powerful feelings.

2. Talk about feelings.

Anger is a typical inclination one can gain when managed appropriately. By recognizing all feelings, from satisfaction and enthusiasm to bitterness, anger, desire, and dissatisfaction, you are teaching your children that they are all pieces of our human collection.

Talk about how you feel and encourage your children to do the same. It will assist them with building up a respectful demeanor towards self as well as other people and structure healthy connections throughout everyday life.

3. Address disappointing behavior serenely, however solidly.

Children act mischievously at times. That is a part of growing up. Talk to them in a firm manner that leaves their pride intact, yet clarifies that specific behaviors are unacceptable.

Get down to their eye level instead of speaking to them from high up or from far away. Simultaneously, make sure to recognize their respectful behavior and critical thinking.

4. Use results, yet forget about the dangers.

Utilizing dangers with discipline makes for progressively furious sentiments, hatred, and conflict. Over the long haul, they keep your child from creating internal self-control. Threats and punishment embarrass and disgrace children, causing them to feel uncertain. Then again, results that address a specific behavior, however, accompany reasonable scolding (like removing a toy in the wake of clarifying that toys are for playing, not for hitting) assist children with deciding to make better decisions.

A word on fundamental needs.

Having their essential needs met, similar to rest and appetite, keeps children happy, and makes for better behavior in general. Additionally, setting up schedules will assist them with being less restless and diminish the danger of misbehaving.

What to do when you yell.

Regardless of how great your yelling counteraction system is, in some cases, you will speak more loudly. That is OK. Be ready to apologize, and your children will become familiar with a significant exercise: We all commit errors, and we have to apologize. On the off chance that your children yell, help them to remember the limits, and how yelling is not a satisfactory method for communication. They need to realize you are prepared to tune in as long as they show respect. Model this by permitting yourself an opportunity to cool your jets before talking to your children when your anger overpowers you.

You will assist them with making deep-rooted tendencies that make conflict management simpler. That will show your children to comprehend the mix-ups, theirs, and other people's, and that forgiveness is an essential tool for healthy communication in a family. If, so far, you have depended on yelling to discipline your children, and you are most likely observing its impacts:

- Your children may rely on shouting to convey the desired information to one another.

- They talk back and even yell at you as opposed to talking respectfully.

- Your association with them is unsteady and unpredictable to the point of not having the option to converse healthily.

- They may pull away from you and become more affected by their companions than you.

You can change all that. Start by having an open talk with your children about the irrationality of yelling and why showing your anger that way is not healthy. Make your home a quiet environment where individuals speak with respect and recognize each other's emotions without accusing, disgracing, or judging. Candid accountability keeps the discourse open and keeps everybody in the family responsible. On the off chance that you commit errors, do not surrender. It is anything but a simple street, yet it merits each action.

Is your anger too profoundly situated?

On the off chance that your anger is frequently spilling onto your children and you experience difficulty remaining calm all the time, perceiving that you have an issue is the initial move toward figuring out how to manage it. This knowledge will assist you with resting easy thinking about yourself and conversing quietly and lovingly with your children. A portion of the signs that point to anger issues include:

- Getting irrationally furious over apparently minor issues.

- Experiencing stress-related side effects like hypertension, stomach distress, or uneasiness.

- Feeling liable and sad after an anger episode, yet seeing the instance repeating frequently.

- Engaging in conflicts with others as opposed to having respectful exchanges.

A counselor can likewise assist you with creating methods to try to avoid panicking and prevent upheavals and help you with improving the harming impacts of anger on your association with your friends and family.

Yelling at your kids can damage their brains, just as it can harm their ears.

Yelling at children can fundamentally and forever adjust the structure of their brains. It was an over the top self-constraint - of the sort I never show towards my kids - that stopped me from walking them straight off for a brain examination. Is yelling at one's children a definitively unthinkable parental act? Admittedly, it negates all the great parenting mottos. Yelling at children affords them that you are "crazy".

Interestingly, nearly everybody appears to do it. Once upon a time, before in my career as a writer, I discovered such an eager line of volunteer interviewees. What is more, nearly everybody admits that it does not work.

Yelling at your children to obey resembles utilizing the horn to control your vehicle - and it creates similar outcomes. However, this overlooks what is essential: you do not yell at your kids because, after careful thought, you consider it the best methodology; you yell at them since you have lost your cool. The triggers are numerous and different, yet parental disconnection and fatigue come high on the list. Practically all shouters feel regretful. The best advantage of not having children must be that you can continue accepting that you are a pleasant individual. When you have children, you understand how wars start. Family life is such a cauldron of feelings. A happy family must have some conflict in it: in personal connections, individuals need to argue and makeup. A 15-year-old makes you yell at him at some point or another.

Yelling at kids is regularly divided by smacking them; however, for vast numbers of us, it is another option. Be that as it may, when does yelling transform into tormenting or offensive attack? It is somewhat a matter of degree and proportion. On the off chance that there is no reduction in noise and there is no love also, it is damaging. The age of the child and what you state is likewise significant. A toddler does not comprehend the contrast between you yelling at them and loathing them; he expounds. With a teenager, that is not the situation. There is additionally a distinction between genuine self-revelation ("you have exasperated me") and misuse ("you are a terrible little imp").

Even though vast numbers of us stress that yelling at our children will damage their brains as well as their development, most children immediately become desensitized to boisterous parents and tune out. The more you yell, the less they tune in. Thus, the stronger you need to yell as the years pass by - discouraging, would you say? Another aftereffect of yelling at children is that they become quite proficient shouters themselves. Then again, children who have never been yelled at can be very delicate flowers (or so I like to think). Also, practically all shouters concur that a decent yell can dispel any stale air and be freeing.

One method for yelling less is to record your nightly dinner on tape and hear it back a short time later: It can be very enlightening. Pondering the trigger circumstances can help. Is it when your glucose level is low, or theirs is? Is it generally when you get them from school? You can likewise do whatever it takes not to become involved with their anger. Most significantly, moms shift in the degree to which they can endure

15

and manage the conflict incited by loving and loathing a similar child. The blame and nervousness we feel about yelling at our kids come halfway from our uneasiness with the elements of parenting, and disillusionment at neglecting to turn into the romanticized parents we trusted we would be. No one would advocate yelling as attractive parental behavior; however, it may be an increasingly practical point that it is not such a considerable effort to attempt to staunch it as to recognize it.

Talking to Your Child After You Yell.

Almost every parent loses control and shouts at their children from time to time. Be that as it may, imagine a scenario in which you do it over and again. Scientists presume parents are yelling more. Parents have been shaped to abstain from beating, so they vent their anger and disappointment by yelling. Three out of four parents shout or yell at their children or teenagers about once every month, on average, for acting up or frustrating them. Progressively, specialists and parenting specialists are honing in on how it harms a child, just as how to stop it. Raising your voice is not, in every case, awful. Uproariously portraying an issue can point it out without harming anybody. Yelling becomes harming when it is an individual assault, deprecating, or accusing a child with proclamations, for example, "How did you not know that?" or, "You do not understand anything!"

Numerous parents lose control when they think about children's misbehavior or insubordination. They feel assaulted or think the child's activities show inadequacy on them. Parents who consider these negative feelings as surprising, overpowering, and upsetting will, in general, feel progressively undermined and baffled with each new turmoil, says an investigation distributed not long ago in the Journal of Family Psychology. This example, called "emotional flooding," triggers a dwindling in the relationship, upsetting the parent's critical thinking capacity and filling emotional responses, for instance, yelling.

Teenagers whose parents use "cruel verbal discipline, for example, yelling or put-downs, are bound to have behavior issues and gloomy side effects. Numerous parents lose control because they think about children's misbehavior literally. What can help: figuring out how to see the warning signs in your body, having age-appropriate expectations for your child, and building a buffer into everyday schedules to enable time to manage mistakes? Another study proposes that yelling at children may have outcomes that go past those of physical abuse. Eight-year-olds whose parents disciplined them by yelling, has fewer fulfilling associations with emotional partners and life partners at age 23, as indicated by another investigation. Parents who yell may pass up an opportunity to instruct children to direct their feelings appropriately.

Abuse additionally indicated less fulfilling grown-up connections; however, the negative impacts counterbalanced when parents praised their children on different occasions. The negative implications of yelling were not removed by parental warmth, in any case. The negative critical thinking strategies that children internalize when their parents yell may stay with them as grown-ups. Children additionally may anticipate that others should negatively treat them, and unknowingly pick partners who satisfy that need.

Yelling is the place 90% of us do the most damage. Parents can figure out how to see signs that a blowup is preparing and dial down their stress. Cautioning signs can include tightness in the throat or chest, shallow or quick breathing, and a tightening of the teeth or jaw, negative thoughts about oneself, or sentiments of being overpowered. Construct a buffer of extra time into everyday schedules to permit time for minor setbacks, for example, spilled milk or lost coats. Figuring out how to begin sentences with "I" instead of "you" can assist parents with moving from a furious assault to a teaching minute.

Parents can transform a disaster into a chance to learn by including kids in discovering answers for the hidden issue. Saying 'sorry' can help fix the relationship after the turmoil and set a positive model. Numerous parents explode because they have unrealistic expectations; for example, expecting a two-year-old not to push parental buttons on parenting issues, including discipline. We state to our children, 'Behave,' and indeed, they are. Not expecting that children should be perfect, or almost along these lines, can quiet parents' dissatisfactions. So this can be considered to be a disappointment or as an open door for him to learn.

Parents can transform a disaster into a teaching moment by including kids in finding solutions. Sitting tight for a quiet minute and expressing the expectation the child violated. At that point, give the child the decision about how to keep the misbehavior from happening again. Welcoming a child to find solutions shows critical thinking skills.

CHAPTER TWO

THE NEED TO EDUCATE YOUR CHILD AT AN EARLY AGE.

Lots of people have second thoughts about the significance of pre-kindergarten education. Children who enrolled in preschool tend to act more maturely and have higher IQ scores after entering kindergarten than their friends without formal training at that age. Similarly, it was indicated that children who attended Head Start programs adapted better than children not enrolled.

Pundits of pre-kindergarten education guarantee the contrasts between children enrolled in pre-school, and children not enrolled in formal education are just perceivable during kindergarten, first, and second grade. During the ensuing years, children who have not gotten formal education preceding kindergarten test at a similar level and carry on like their friends with pre-kindergarten formal education. Hence, Head Start children might be at an advantage for two or three years; however, from that point forward, their colleagues perform at similar levels.

Another serious issue with Head Start programs is that families footing the bill for these projects typically originate from families living underneath the poverty line, so these projects are not promptly accessible for children from all foundations. In any case, children can get a formal education in different manners other than Head Start programs, including childcare and parents teaching their little youngsters. Even though children in childcare projects can grow mentally, children advance most when parents remain at home with their children and educate them.

Most childhood education authorities guarantee that small kids adapt best when they are not pushed excessively hard, when they have a chance to interact with their friends, and when their parents and teachers treat them sympathetically. Likewise, children adapt best when guidance and educational exercises are just a small part of their days. This is particularly valid for children attending pre-school programs since it is not beneficial for small kids to be isolated from their parents for extraordinarily long timeframes. Children, for the most part, do not benefit from programs with inexperienced instructors and enormous classroom sizes.

Children in education at an early age ordinarily advance in the following manners: improved social skills, less or no requirement for specialized curriculum guidance during ensuing school years, better grades, and upgraded abilities to focus. In like manner, a few analysts have presumed that youngsters that were enrolled in pre-school programs frequently move on from secondary school, go to school, have fewer behavioral issues, and do not get associated with misconduct in their youth and young adult years.

The discovery detailing these benefits was completed during the '80s. Notwithstanding benefiting children facing typical development, it was additionally demonstrated that children with learning or other developmental issues benefit tremendously from pre-kindergarten education. Likewise, children with parents deeply engaged with their pre-kindergarten education do not experience similar positive outcomes from Head Start programs as children originating from homes where it is not as much an accentuation. Children encouraged how to communicate in a second language during their initial formative years are likewise in a superior situation to learn English at a young age.

Numerous individuals do not feel the government ought to decide if children ought to be required to get formal pre-kindergarten education. One purpose behind this is children who are educated by their parents during their initial formative years experience the same benefits from children who were enrolled in pre-school programs, particularly children getting much care from parents. Parents choosing to educate their children themselves should use imaginative thoughts and exercises while instructing them.

Regardless of the distinctions in sentiment about formal pre-kindergarten education, children profit by getting some education during their initial formative years. Be that as it may, there is no one-size-fits-all guidance most appropriate for all children. While a few children benefit significantly from pre-school, it may not be the best educational setting for all children. Much of the time, children benefit most by getting educational guidance from their parents. Parents must assess a child's unique character before figuring out which program is most appropriate for a child since not all projects similarly benefit children.

The Value of Early Childhood Education.

Most children start getting formal education during kindergarten. Later analytical research has demonstrated that learning and mental advancement start following birth. During the initial three years of a child's life, essential brain and neural advancement happen. In this way, children enormously benefit from receiving an education before kindergarten. Since kindergarten starts around the ages of 5 to 6 for most children, after significant brain advancement happens, parents should start teaching children at younger ages.

Numerous parents start instructing their children during these significant formative years. Be that as it may, numerous parents disregard the effort to educate their children. Numerous variables can add to this, for example, long work hours and lack of knowledge about the significance of teaching children at a young age.

Unfortunately, not entirely are children negatively influenced by not being educated at an early age. However, the negative impacts regularly resound through society. A test assessed at two groups of children for an all-inclusive timeframe, those with formal pre-school education and those not getting any proper education. As indicated by their discoveries, children with formal education scored higher on reading tests during the resulting school years. It was additionally demonstrated that the children who did not get any proper education in their pre-kindergarten years were bound to battle with substance abuse and degenerate behaviors in their initial grown-up years.

The ends drawn from most research about early childhood education are that people and social orders enormously advantage, as far as social, monetary, and different benefits, from it. The more noteworthy emphasis put on early education is one methodology to mitigate substance abuse and criminal behavior that troubles numerous teenagers and youthful adults. The monetary benefits, for instance, can be colossal when the emphasis is put on early childhood education.

It is vain to set up government educational goals without pre-kindergarten education programs. Therefore, it is associated with a political battle known as Born Learning; a crusade intended to encourage parents to start teaching children at a young age. The United Way works with parents who feel ill-equipped or incapable of educating their small kids effectively. For instance, since children have low capacities to focus, parents are encouraged to utilize daily schedule exercises to show children significant lessons, for example, requesting that a child go into a room and recover a predefined measure of things. This enables small kids to get comfortable with numbers and figure out how to add. Different tasks, for example, having children recognize the colors and shapes of objects, is another effective action to educate them.

Improving the pre-kindergarten education of children is one step that can be taken to improve the general public financially and socially. It has been indicated that children should start to get an education before kindergarten since children experience generous brain development during these early years.

The Most Important Money Lessons To Teach Your Kids.

Given how vital monetary skills are to navigating life, it is astonishing that our schools do not show children how to handle money. As a parent, in any case, you can teach your child significant budgetary lessons — and you should. The sooner parents start using explicit everyday instruction about money (for instance, allow a six-year-old $2 and let her pick which vegetable to purchase), the happier our kids will be. Parents are the main impact on their children's money related behaviors, so it is dependent upon us to raise the age of careful purchasers, financial specialists, savers, and suppliers.

The following are the top money lessons to be scholarly at each age, just as exercises to outline each point.

Ages 2-5.

The Lesson: You may need to wait to purchase something you need.

This is a hard idea for individuals to learn. In any case, the capacity to delay satisfaction can likewise anticipate how successful one will be as an adult. Kids at this age need to discover that on the off chance that they genuinely need something, they should pause and save to get it.

Money lessons at this age set the pace for later on. You truly cannot begin too soon. At the point when we go into a store, if I state, 'We do not have cash for this,' they are smart — they realize we have Visas. So, one would say, "We are here to purchase a present for X, and we are not going to purchase anything for you since we are not here for

24

that". Kids at that point rapidly discover that going into a store does not always mean you will purchase something for them.

Exercises For Ages 2 To 5.

1. At the point when your child is waiting in line, say, to go on the swings, talk about the fact that it is so critical to figure out how to hang tight for what the individual in question needs.

2. Make three containers – each marked "Saving," "Spending," or "Sharing". Every time your child gets cash, regardless of whether for doing tasks or from a birthday, separate the money similarly among the containers. Have them utilize the spending container for little buys, similar to treat or stickers. Money in the sharing box can go to somebody you know who needs it or be used to give to a friend's needs. The saving container ought to be for increasingly costly items.

3. Have your child define an objective, for example, to purchase a toy. Ensure it is not all that expensive that they will not have the option to bear the cost of it for a considerable length of time. "At that point, it just gets frustrating, and it gets difficult for them to wait. It is extremely increasingly about her being mindful that she is putting something aside for an objective than, Oh, I truly need her to figure out how to use $10 to purchase the tutu.' You need to set them up for progress. On the off chance that your child has a costly objective, think of a coordinating project to assist her with arriving at it in a sensible time allotment. (While a reward is an individual decision for each family, at this age, a little

allowance could enable a child to put something aside for these objectives).

Each time your child adds cash to the reserve funds container, assist her with checking up the amount she has, talk with her about the amount she needs to contact her objective, and when she will arrive at it. Each one of those behaviors is hugely a good time for kids. Furthermore, it gives them a feeling of the significance of waiting and being patient and saving.

Ages 6-10.

The Lesson: You have to profit.

At this age, it is imperative to disclose to your child that cash is limited, and it is critical to settle on smart decisions because once you go through the cash you have, you do not have more to spend. While at this age, you ought to likewise stay aware of lessons like the saving, spending and sharing containers, and objective setting, you ought to likewise start to engage your child in increasingly grown-up money related essential leadership.

Exercises For Ages 6 To 10.

1. Remember your child for some monetary choices. For example, clarify the option with "I picked these grapes as opposed to the brand name is because it costs 50 pennies less and tastes the same to me. Alternatively, talk about agreements, for example, purchasing regular staples like paper towels in mass to get a less expensive per-thing cost.

2. Give your child some cash, like $2, in a store and have her settle on decisions about what fruit or vegetable to purchase, inside the parameters of what you need, to give them the experience of profiting.

3. When you are shopping, talk out loud about how you are settling on your money related choices as an adult, posing questions like, "Is this something we outrageously need? Or, on the other hand, would we be able to skip it this week since we are going out to dinner?" "Would I be able to get it?" "Would it cost less elsewhere? Might we be able to go to another store and get two of these rather than one for the same price?"

Ages 11-13.

The Lesson: The sooner you save, the quicker your cash can grow from accumulating funds.

At this age, you can move from putting something aside for temporary objectives to long haul objectives. Present the idea of progressive growth, when you obtain interest both on your reserve funds just as on past, the excitement from your investment funds.

Exercises For Ages 11 To 13.

1. Depict accumulating funds using exact numbers, since asking about them shows this is more effective than depicting it in theory. Clarify, "On the off chance that you put aside $100 consistently beginning at age 14, you would have $23,000

by age 65; however, if you start at age 35, you will just have $7,000 by age 65".

2. Have your child do some accruing funds estimations. Here, she can perceive how much cash she will acquire on the off chance that she contributes a specific sum, and it develops by a particular cost of financing. What is more, have her learn from an interesting case of somebody who utilized self-multiplying dividends to his advantage inconceivably well.

3. Have your child define a more drawn out time objective for something more costly than the toys she may have been putting something aside for. Those sorts of tradeoffs, called opportunity costs — what are the things you're offering up to set aside cash — is a beneficial thing to talk about? At this age, kids are attempting not to save since they need to purchase stuff, yet considering what long term objectives are and what they are giving up shows that it is a decent choice. For instance, if your child has a propensity for purchasing a snack after school each day, she may choose, she would preferably put that cash toward an iPad.

Ages 14-18.

The Lesson: When looking at universities, make sure to think about how much each school would cost.

Search for the "net value number cruncher" on school websites to perceive the extra expenses other than tuition. Be that as it may, do not let the sticker price discourage your child. Show them the salaries of school graduates vs. that of individuals without college educations, making it a profitable venture.

Exercises For Ages 14 To 18.

1. Talk about the amount you can add to your child's tuition every year. Each parent should begin the school year with a discussion about cost by ninth grade. Handling the subject early and speaking the truth about what your family can bear the cost of will assist kids with being practical about where they may apply. Be that as it may, remember that there are numerous approaches to college other than with your very own cash. With your child, investigate which non-public schools are liberal with scholarships, its amount is in free money, for example, awards and grants, how much in credits that your child should repay, and what government projects can assist pay with sponsorships.

2. Have your child utilize the College Scorecard to analyze how every school costs, what the work opportunities of graduates are, and how many students get advanced positions could influence your child's way of life after graduation on the off chance that the person went to that school. Similarly, as with any speculation, examine together whether the cash put in will pay off in the end.

3. Gauge your monetary guide and research extra credits, grants, and awards — and use financial analysts to evaluate month to month advance installments. Get some answers concerning

credit reimbursement alternatives, which restricts your regularly scheduled payments to only 10% of your optional pay.

Parents ought to make their school kids find a low maintenance line of work, including that analysis, shows that students who work 20 hours every week or less at places of employment improve grades since they are increasingly engaged in student life. In any case, limit those hours! Working over 20 hours out of every week can hurt kids' scholarly achievement.

Ages 18+.

The Lesson: You should utilize a credit card just on the off chance that you can take care of the payments in full every month.

It is effortless to slide into credit card debt, which could give your child the weight of taking care of Mastercard debt simultaneously with tuition. Besides, it could influence their credit score, which could make it hard to save, purchase a vehicle or a home, or even find a new line of work. In some cases, proposed businesses check credit.

The average family unit owes $7,084 in credit card obligation. To alter the course of spending too far in the red and piling on several dollars per year in interest, parents must show their kids how to utilize credit cards mindfully (or even better—not in any way!— except if they can cover the full balance consistently).

Exercises For Ages 18+.

1. Show a child that if a parent cosigns on a charge card, any late payment could likewise influence the parent's record of loan repayment.

2. Together, search for a charge card that offers a low financing cost and no yearly expense.

3. Clarify that it is significant not to charge ordinary things because, on the off chance that you have an emergency cost that you cannot cover with savings, you can charge that. In any case, it is best to save, in any event, three months of everyday costs for an emergency fund. However, six to nine months' worth is perfect. Figure out how to save for an emergency fund.

Key Benefits of Early Childhood Education.

At the point when children are young, they are learning. Each new experience, each word they adapt, each behavior they embrace, is an interest in an increasingly productive future. You can never have a more noticeable impact on an individual than when they are in their initial childhood years. Most parents have, in every case, innately understood this, and the Government is beginning to make up for the lost time.

Early childhood education is tied in with sharpening and embellishment the all-encompassing child, which will, in the long-run structure, the premise of their deep-rooted excursion. From an expert experience of years as a preschool educator, I have recognized 13 essential benefits of early childhood education:

1. Socialization:

Socialization with individuals other than the child's family in a protected environment is a fundamental primary component to the underneath territories. As parents, we instinctively comprehend that it is essential to familiarize our children with other children and bolster their progress into their community get-togethers. The earlier we do this, the better, as it assists children with defeating shyness and additional self-certainty. On the off chance that we do not do this for an excessively long time, we block their social development.

2. The idea of Cooperation:

Figuring out how to share, coordinate, alternate, and drive forward inside a protected learning environment, guided by experts who have the children's ultimate benefits on the most fundamental level. This is particularly significant for the oldest child, who may not be accustomed to imparting to their kin at home - while it very well may be a troublesome exercise, it is so vital to learning it early.

3. Empowering Holistic Development:

The method taken to produce a solid establishment for a child's emotional, social, physical, and mental advancement, will set them up for a lifetime. Early childhood teachers are prepared to recognize areas where support is required for every child and building projects and exercises around these. Their friends are likewise critical in such manner, as preschoolers are typically useful, helpful, and comprehensive.

4. Excitement for Lifelong Learning:

Lessons ought to be given in a fun and energizing ways that will encourage children to be competent students. We have to motivate a hunger for learning with eagerness and excitement. Love of education-for reading, learning, revelation, nature-flourishes in preschool.

5. Pass on the Value of Education Through Experience:

Getting a handle on the assessment of learning and education by setting a model as good examples and by giving genuine encounters. While parents will consistently be the most significant effect on a child's initial life, acquainting them with a preschool environment gives them another point of view on the significance of education that will stay with them all through their school career. It likewise shows that you respect their education remarkably.

6. Respect:

Teaching the belief of respect for other people isn't restricted to individuals and things. However, it can likewise mean respect for their environment, both immediate and worldwide. There is no better spot to get familiar with these ideas than in a wild preschool environment, where everything is shared, and consideration and habits are both instructed and adapted naturally.

7. Collaboration:

Exhibiting and imparting the significance of collaboration that can show respect for the assessments of others, listening, participation, and correspondence. Numerous preschool exercises revolve around cooperation for this very explanation; an individual who figures out how to function in a group at an early age will eventually be all the more socially adjusted and increasingly employable!

8. Flexibility:

Significantly, early childhood educators and parents cooperate to create strength in children in flexibility, as could be expected under the circumstances. By making a reliable, secure, and reasonable social environment, with precise expectations and reliable outcomes, children can create skills in managing themselves and their feelings. It is an educator's business to give a trustworthy environment where children can learn through direct experiences. They may experience bumps, bruises, or losing a game every once in a while. However, this is the establishment for building adapting techniques for more noteworthy difficulties throughout everyday life.

9. Focus:

During the preschool years, children investigate at each chance to find new experiences, new companions, and new environments. Their brains are energetic and creative. As early childhood teachers, we have to offset this get-up-and-go with the capacity to tune in, follow directions, take care of tasks and take part in exercises to build up the essential fundamental ability of concentration.

10. Tolerance:

Consistently as grown-ups, we experience circumstances where our patience is exercised. Children need chances to be connected with a bounty of social experiences, where they can investigate and rehearse the social aptitude of persistence. By teaching through modeling, job demonstrating, and social experiences, children can build up their understanding and figure out how to wait for their turn. Models from the preschool setting incorporate sharing an instructor's attention, a toy, the play area, or waiting in line for a game.

12. Certainty and Self-Esteem:

A solid feeling of prosperity provides children with certainty, positive thinking, and self-esteem, which will encourage children to examine their gifts, skills, and premiums. Positive cooperations with other children and instructors will advance a positive, healthy, and secure perspective on themselves that will enable them to move toward circumstances and issues unquestionably for the duration of their lives.

13. Introduction to Diversity:

Appreciating contrast and variety are essential to a child's initial improvement. Early childhood education serves to direct children to acknowledge and acknowledge contrasts and become balanced supporters of society. Significantly, children comprehend that everybody is unique in their specific manner with their own culture, convictions, and ethnicity.

Preschool is far beyond playing. While the essential educational benefits of preschool, (for example, proficiency and numeracy) are substantial, the advances children accomplish towards turning out to be balanced people are genuinely priceless. Kindly, do not let your child pass up this unique chance.

CHAPTER THREE

EFFECTIVE COMMUNICATION: HOW TO TALK TO AND LISTEN TO YOUR TODDLER.

Grown-ups frequently become baffled when communicating with little youngsters. Parents and educators regularly ask me, "Would we say we are truly communicating? Do they get me? Do I genuinely get them?" Children, particularly little youngsters, are as yet figuring out how to utilize words. Their communication skills are moderately new. The language might be the last piece included as a child tackles the riddle of communications. Learning words and sentences are a lot harder range of abilities than mimicry or motioning.

Parents, for the most part, comprehend their newborn child's needs from the infant's outward appearance, or the tone of their cry. Afterward, grown-ups see more clearly nonverbal communication in children and encourage them. For instance, most young parents adapt rapidly to what the "small" move resembles and hurry to push the child to potty-train. For a little youngster, it very well may be simpler to utilize body language or show feelings, than to attempt to locate the correct words. For a toddler, language can be a cumbersome, mentally devouring point of view.

The issue is exacerbated if the child is continually revised with "useful" correctness, for example, "No, that word is pronounced..." or "Didn't you intend to say...?" Even as grown-ups, we are once in a while at a misfortune for the correct words. In an emotionally or physically overpowering circumstance, words can fail us. For a small kid attempting to convey, that can be an everyday battle. Numerous young students experience issues with the subtleties of language. For instance, "two" and "too" sound the same yet mean various things. In like manner, your manner of speaking when saying, "Gracious, incredible," can change the aim of the words. Your outward appearance - attempting to keep a straight face while reprimanding a child - can build your communication challenges with children.

Little youngsters are figuring out how words are utilized and what they mean in various settings. Be that as it may until they believe that they have it right, they might be hesitant to used words. As of late, we have seen incredible advances in working with childhood communication troubles. Some communication alternatives for children incorporate gesture-based communication for preverbal children. This constructs their communication skills and certainty while they are figuring out how to utilize words.

Remember these tips when communicating with children, all things considered:

1. Continuously talk during an age-appropriate way to a child.

2. Never mistake that for speaking down or condescendingly. Children will know/sense it.

3. Search for all the various ways the child is communicating. This may recall changes for tendencies. The person may utilize drawings or doodles to express feelings. Or on the other hand, you may see expanded affectability or withdrawal.

4. On the off chance that it is more secure for them to talk through an invisible friend or stuffed animal, enable them to so. Listen when a child says, "My friend Johnny says..." or "Kitty-cat doesn't like...".

5. Try not to attempt to rush communications, or push a child to talk until the individual in question is prepared to.

6. Before talking with your child, consistently ensure you are in a loving, responsive temperament. Never judge. Utilize each chance to show your child how to think, not what to think.

It is not unexpected to feel baffled when communicating with small kids. It does not imply that both of you have a communication issue. By understanding the communication challenges that little kids face, you can discover approaches to talk, verbally, and nonverbally.

The most effective method to Talk with Young Children.

As a parent, you may consider what you can do to enable your child to learn *how* to talk. Incredibly, most children usually procure language just by the everyday experiences of listening to others talk. Parents, at times, attempt to "jump-start" their child's communication in various ways. A portion of these ways intuitively are useful; different strategies may discourage children from attempting to talk. As opposed to displaying things you ought not to do, let me share with you three strategies that I use as a discourse language pathologist to advance language improvement. You may perceive that you are now utilizing these strategies naturally without acknowledging it! Let me encourage you to invest some energy every day, utilizing these communication strategies with your child.

The principal mechanism accessible to you is to recognize and rehash what your child is stating, however, including slightly more data to what your child said. For instance, if your child says "du" for "juice," and you realize that your child is mentioning more, you can say "need more squeeze? This will give extra data about how to articulate "juice," just as to show extended sentence structure. This strategy is known as "extension" and is a useful idea for parents to comprehend. (Coincidentally, this does exclude desire for your child rehashing back your words like a parrot! You are just giving extra data - a grin - with regards to a normally happening occasion).

The other tool you can utilize is to say about what you are doing, or what your child is doing, while the occasion or action is going on. Once more, this does not include anticipating that your child should rehash anything. It necessarily implies that you are giving a verbal story of what's going on. I would recommend keeping your sentences short for toddlers or preschoolers who are speaking in phrases, and to utilizing single words or two-word phrases for children who are merely starting to express with single words. You may think about this as portraying an occasion.

A third device is to comprehend, acknowledge, and delight in the articulation that your child is utilizing during their speaking endeavors. Time after time, parents endeavors to address their children's discourse, with the impact of debilitating speaking or transforming it into a control issue. By recognizing your comprehension of what your child is stating, and re-expressing the words (as referenced above), you improve the probability of your child's longing to continue talking. We genuinely need communication among you and your child to be a charming occasion. Formative elocution is the way children learn!

Speaking and Listening to Problem Toddler.

An issue toddler presents numerous difficulties to a grown-up. Simply the expression "issue toddler" has negative ramifications and can make one incorrectly hear the child. Significantly, grown-ups keep up the balance while speaking and listening to issue toddler. On the off chance that an adult isn't open and attempting to be reasonable, at that point, the child is at a disadvantage from the beginning, and that never is a decent circumstance for anybody. The facts confirm that if you anticipate cynicism, you will, in general, get it.

At the point when you talk and tune in to issue toddler, recall whom you are speaking with. A child is only a "grown-up in preparing," and they ought to be managed all things considered. They are learning, and you are there to educate them. If you utilize this methodology, things won't run over so unpalatably, and you will have the option to react in a higher amount of an educational way than a disciplinary one. Children need to figure out how to convey what their needs are to get the outcomes they are searching for, and they likewise need to comprehend that regardless of an individual's age, we do not generally get things how we need them. Letting a child see this, disclosing it to them can go far in quieting a problematic circumstance.

A toddler does not generally have the perception of the words we need to use to clarify something, yet we can utilize activities to help conquer any hindrance. Show them through your actions that you are listening to them. That consoles them that somebody is listening to them. You must carry discussions to their level when you are speaking and listening to issue toddlers. Attempt to see how they are deciphering the words you express, or what they mean by what they state. Understanding this can enable you to know where you have to alter your terms.

Speaking and listening to issue toddlers or any children besides, can be a challenging assignment for some grown-ups. Grown-ups can get overpowered by merely communicating with only adults. A child may want to talk to an outsider; however, with a little exertion, you can effectively convey. Make sure to be patient and let the child talk, do not anticipate that they should carry on a discussion as a grown-up would, let them state what they have to say, hear them out, and afterward give them how they have to hear you out consequently. Doing this will help make your communications simpler while they are youthful, and it will likewise place them on the correct street for discussion effectively as a grown-up.

The Golden Keys To Communication.

The breakdown in communication among Mother and Child does not start with the beginning of youth, as we might want to accept. From the time your children are newborn, they are attempting to get you to comprehend their needs, needs, emotions, and thoughts. The accompanying tips apply whether you're a parent trying to speak with your teenagers or newborn children. It began way back with attempting to untangle your child's infant talk, correct? In any case, trust me, this stuff works. On the off chance that you try these principles of engagement, the connections you have with your children will be perpetually changed, and your day by day life will feel colossally upgraded.

1. Tune in. Eliminate all interruptions if possible. Having an environment helpful for listening is significantly effective in communication. Your child should feel that they have your full focus, and you need to feel the equivalent. You will not generally have the chance to control the volume in your environment. Despite everything, you have the alternative of moving with your child to a calmer space.

2. Be Open. On the off chance that you get together with assumptions and decisions, trust me, your child will understand them intuitively, and communication will right away decay. Come into the discussion with a receptive outlook so you can hear and be on top of what it is your child is attempting to let you know. This doesn't imply that you need to concur or surrender; it just means you have given free space for communication.

3. Approve. Everybody needs to realize that their emotions, thoughts, and assessments are significant and esteemed. Along these lines, while your child is talking to you or communicating, pause for a minute to rehash what they have said and ask them, 'Did I get that right?' Then, portray a portion of the hidden emotions they may have dependent on what they have communicated. In case you're managing a crying infant or toddler, something very similar applies. Tell them that you comprehend why they are upset, you would like them to be happy again and that they will be alright. Approval of your child's sentiments is incredibly noteworthy in building their self-certainty and self-esteem.

4. Bargain. In opposition to mainstream thinking, trading off does not need to be a back-and-forth. After you hear each out other's point of view and convey lovingly, offer a few different ways to haggle with your child, so both of your needs are met, if conceivable. As a dependable parent, there will frequently be times when you shouldn't allow any of the things your child has mentioned. Instead you can recommend some safe options that are healthy and satisfactory for them to choose. Consequently, request that your child focuses on giving you a portion of your needs. This is particularly identified with discussions that parents have with their teenagers. Adolescents are typically battling with their self-character and autonomy. Discover harmony between understanding your child's needs and haggling without gambling responsibility. Contingent upon your child's development, you can decide the degree of the room you offer them to choose.

5. Body Language. A parent's body language can send the hardest criminal into tears. Children immediately become touchy to their parent's look of dissatisfaction or frustration. If you need the discussion to work out in the right way, ensure your body language is specific and inviting. Continuously keep in touch with your children while you are negotiating. It encourages excellent communication tendencies, and it expresses that you are not kidding about what you are stating. Abstain from folding your arms and legs as it is amazingly representative of protectiveness and hardheadedness. Sit upright and look mindful so your children will realize you are centered around what they are stating. What's more, if you don't mind whatever you do...do not feign exacerbation except if you need to experience the boomerang effect. Children will impersonate how you manage worry in testing times. Along these lines, parents, be specific and mindful of your body language when communicating with your child.

6. Tone. Screaming at your children turns them off and shuts them down. If they experience it at home, they will convey it to any place they go. Attempt to demonstrate healthy behavior during trying discussions by keeping your volume at a quiet level. This will show your child that you're still in charge and are not responsive. Your tone sets the temperament of the discussion, yet it also impacts how your children will connect and act in the public eye. Thus, address your child in the manner in which you would need them to treat others - with adoration and respect.

7. Demeanor. Nobody wants to associate with an individual who has an awful disposition. Something very similar goes for your children. They won't have any desire to have a dialog with you on the off chance that they feel your attitude is negative or sense strain. Attempt to discharge all the negative feelings and thoughts you have with the circumstance first so you can talk and tune in with a clear head and loving heart.

8. Genuineness. Show your kids how to be straightforward by being straightforward with them. Also, your child's memory is far keener than your own! At the time when you make promises, ensure you're ready to hold up your end of the deal. In case you're untrustworthy with your children, you encourage them not exclusively to be selfish with you and to others also. The subject of genuineness among parents and children is a sensitive one. You should utilize your best judgment here. Children trust their parents more than any other person on earth from the time they take in their first breath of air. As a parent, you must be sensitive to your child's trust and certainty. At the point when it is broken on your part, they will search out approaches to fix the hurt that may not be beneficial or safe.

9. Approach with Love. In case you're originating from a position of adoration, the individual you're talking to will feel it and be open. Everybody characteristically needs to be adored and feel loved. They continuously attempt to speak and act with altruism and care. Generally, individuals are responsive. If somebody is communicating adoration to us, we will restore the angle and be open to healthy communication.

The Most Effective Method to Discipline Your Child Without Smacking or Shouting.

If you have a toddler, aged 2-4 years, you may think about how it looks if you wound up conquered to an individual 33% your size. For certain children, the 'terrible twos and past' stage comprises of naughty curiosity and a couple of episodes of obstinate refusal to do as you inquire. For other children, it might be an instance of temper tantrums, hitting, gnawing, and bedtime craziness. They seem to have no discipline at all.

At the point when your child isn't listening to you, and their behavior is crazy, you can, as a parent, feel as if you are doing everything incorrectly. You may be led to feel like a terrible parent, similar to your child, wouldn't act so severely on the off chance that you were a superior parent. That is a weird inclination to have, and it just erodes your certainty and causes you to feel overpowered, which only exacerbates things.

It is most likely more terrible when you go out with your child, shopping, or to see family and companions, and you can't get them to hear you out. You are always apprehensive that they will have a tantrum, and afterward, everybody will pass judgment on you for not being able to control your child. You may even resort to paying off your child, with the goal that they can maintain good manners. Notwithstanding, with the correct way to deal with teaching your child, you could be back in charge by and by.

All children are extraordinary, and there is unknown clarification for a toddler's sudden wave of terrible behavior. Out of this world on their own and test their recently discovered freedom, their behavior can transform from that of a serene child to one whose behavior is unruly.

As children experience various stages, they are continually trying points of restraint, extending their viewpoints, and attempting to assume responsibility for themselves. Parents need to know the formative stage of their child and afterward set points of control. Note that the breaking points won't work on the off chance that they are not suitable to the child's formative stage. If you are having issues with your toddler, there are some discipline strategies you can use to make your life simpler and to all the more effectively impart the limits to your child. You don't need to depend on screaming or hitting

Before we take a gander at these tips, there is one significant differentiation to make: It is imperative to recognize the child and the behavior. You can tell your child that you don't care for their behavior; however, take care not to oppose them. It is always critical to recall that as the behavior you don't care for and not the child.

One method for teaching your children is giving them a break. The trustworthy guideline is one moment for every year, so on the off chance that they are three years of age, they get 3 minutes. When utilizing this procedure, it is critical to give your child a warning first, and if they proceed with the behavior, at that point, take them to a timeout. Explain to the child precisely why you are having them take a timeout, and once completed, disclose to them again why their behavior was not acceptable.

On the off chance that your child quickly quiets down after they get furious, utilize a 'break.' Have them sit in a seat in the kitchen or front room. Recall you are teaching your child discipline, so don't send them to their room as a discipline, except if there is no other decision. You don't need them to consider their room to be as an awful spot to be, and you might want to watch them as they stew, so you realize they are not breaking things or getting out of hand further.

When teaching your child discipline, give them the rules and directions forthright. Try not to wait until they disrupt the guidelines to clarify the principles. Tell your expectations to children as to what they can do, instead of what they can't do. Or on the other hand, say to them what sort of behavior you need, instead of what you don't need. Utilize plain, clear language. Keep in mind, a toddler is equipped for understanding complex ideas, yet you would prefer not to utilize words they don't comprehend or clarify your prerequisites as a 'cast-off'. Go to the child's level by bowing or getting them, and gradually and cautiously explain what you need them to do.

While teaching your child, don't speak more loudly or hit your child to get them to obey you. Keep an even tone. You may utilize a harsh or firm manner of speaking; however, try to avoid frightening while you are talking. Keep in mind, and you are teaching them how to respond when they are angry or vexed. You would prefer not to fortify this behavior by showing your tantrum. If, when teaching your child, you are in danger of losing control, stop the talk and leave before you do any physical damage.

Attempt to be dependable in the manner you respond to their behavior and attempt to keep that predictable with how they are required to act somewhere else, for example, at school. It is likewise critical to have everybody engaged with caring for your children to have a steady way to deal with discipline. Let your partner, grandparents, or sitters know precisely how you might want your child disciplined and ensure they help it through, and else they will sabotage any advance you have made. Parents ought to never punish their children since this has been shown to have no impact on the child's behavior. The child figures out how to acknowledge the punishing and to endure it, with no enduring impact on the response you needed to change. Probably the ideal methods to encourage excellent behavior is to laud your child when they do share, or when they do head to sleep as you mentioned, or when they finish their dinner. Encouraging feedback can go a long way toward breaking terrible behavioral examples.

CHAPTER FOUR

TEACHING YOUR CHILDREN HEALTHY EMOTIONAL SELF-MANAGEMENT AND CONFLICT RESOLUTION SKILLS.

As a parent, you assume the first job in your child's growth. There are purposeful approaches to grow a healthy parent-child relationship, and developing your child's skills to manage conflict gives an ideal chance.

Conflict occurs in families – between life partners, among kin, and among parents and children. Battling in family life is ordinary and anticipated. How you contend and how you work through issues together can manufacture your child's fundamental abilities with the goal that they are prepared to develop and support healthy connections beyond your family life. Children ages 5-10 should exercise and construct their skills in listening, compassion, communication, and critical thinking to flourish. They should figure out how to stop and cool off before saying or acting in unsafe manners. Furthermore, they'll need to figure out how to consider poor decisions and assume liability for their activities. On the off chance that they cause hurt, parents need to influence children to the next better choice with the goal that they figure out how to retouch physical or emotional damage done.

However, adults as a whole face difficulty in overseeing conflict. "You can't tell me!" your child may shout in shame and disappointment after riding a bicycle into a bustling road. As your child creates, they should test their breaking points and the standards to disguise them. This can prompt battles among parents and their children. Utilizing the means below can help explore this battle with aptitude — the ways below incorporate explicit, viable systems alongside useful, friendly exchanges to set you up.

Why Conflict?

Regardless of whether it's your five-year-old hitting an older sibling in disappointment, your younger child declining to get ready for school, or your nine-year-old arguing plans with a deep-rooted companion, setting up healthy methods for working through conflict that do no mischief to self or others incorporates teaching your child imperative skills that will produce confidence.

Today, for the time being, teaching skills to manage conflict in healthy manners can make:

- More open doors for the relationship, collaboration, and pleasure.

- Trust in one another that we can manage our connections and duties.

- A feeling of prosperity and inspiration to engage.

Tomorrow, in the long haul, overseeing conflict in your child:

- develops a feeling of wellbeing, security, and confidence in self;

- builds skills in self-mindfulness, self-management, social mindfulness, relationship skills, and dependable basic leadership; and

- Deepens family trust and closeness.

Steps for Managing Conflict.

This five-step process can help you and your child to manage conflict. It likewise fabricates significant necessary fundamental abilities in your child. A similar procedure can be utilized to address other parenting issues too. These means are best done when you and your child are not worn out or in a rush. Purposeful communication and effectively constructing a healthy parent relationship will bolster these means.

Stage 1. Get Your Child Thinking by Getting Their Input.

You can get your child pondering, overseeing conflict by asking them open-ended questions. You'll help direct your child's reasoning. You'll additionally start to all the more likely comprehend their considerations, sentiments, and moves identified with how they feel when standing up to difficulties so you can address them. In picking up input, your child:

- Has a more prominent stake in anything they've planned themselves (and with that feeling of proprietorship additionally comes a more noteworthy duty regarding taking care of their issues);

- Has more inspiration to cooperate and coordinate as a result of their feeling of proprietorship;

- Will be working as a team with you on settling on educated choices (understanding the purposes for those choices) about essential parts of their life; and

- Will develop self-control, compassion, and critical thinking skills.

Activities.

Think about what provokes your child in their capacity to manage conflict in healthy manners? For instance, if your child is hurt or feeling dismissed, it's an ordinary reflex for them to lash out in self-protection. Start by thinking about the following.

- Ask about how your child feels when arguing with a family part or companion.

- "What gets you truly annoyed or upset at a friend, a family member?"

- "What emotions do you experience?" (Name the different sentiments that happen).

- "How does your body feel when you're disturbed?" (Name the manners in which that your child physically experiences being vexed whether it's an intensely hot face or a hustling heartbeat).

- "Have you hurt someone else's emotions when you've argued? How did that feel?"

- "How may you have argued differently to express your needs yet not hurt the other individual?"

Stage 2. Show New Skills by Interactive Modeling.

As parents, it's anything but difficult to overlook that children are figuring out how to be in healthy connections, and that incorporates figuring out how to battle reasonably. As a result of your child's learning and advancement, they will settle on missteps and poor decisions. How we, as parents, handle those minutes can decide how we help manufacture their conflict management skills. Finding out about formative achievements can enable a parent to more readily comprehend what their child is experiencing. Here are a few models:

- Five-year-olds are dealing with rules and schedules. Consistency encourages them to feel a feeling of strength.

- Six-year-olds might be progressively well-suited to scrutinize your rules. They blossom with encouragement. They can get reproachful of others and need experience with generosity and inclusion.

- Seven-year-olds need structure and may battle with changes to the agenda. They might be cranky and require consolation from grown-ups.

- Eight-year-olds are stronger when they commit errors. Their companions' and instructors' endorsement is significant.

- Nine-year-olds can turn out to be effectively baffled. They need bearings that contain one guidance. They may stress over friendship support and their very own appearance and interests.

- Ten-year-olds are building up a solid feeling of good and bad and reasonableness. They will, in general, have the option to work through conflicts with friends all the more quickly.

Teaching is not the same as merely telling. Teaching fabricates fundamental skills, develops critical thinking capacities, and sets your child up for progress. Teaching likewise includes demonstrating and rehearsing the positive behaviors you need to see, advancing skills, and forestalling issues. This is additionally a chance to set up significant, intelligent ramifications for when desires are not met.

Activities.

Hang up an image of a traffic light to show valuable conflict management skills as a game. Pretend and make it fun.

Here's the process:

- **RED LIGHT** – Stop and quiet down.

    - Parent: Stand toward one side of the room or yard and turn your back to the players. Have your children get out one common issue they face, and afterward, they can begin running toward you.

    - Flip around to confront them and state, "Stop!" with your handheld out level.

. Now, request that everybody inhale gradually, profoundly, and deeply to work on quieting down.

• **YELLOW LIGHT** – Feel, impart, and think.

. Walk and advance toward you in moderate movement.

. Feel. Children state the issue and how they feel about it. Parents can react by rethinking what their children said into an "I-message, for example, "I feel disappointed when you take my school supplies since I have to utilize them".

. Communicate. Set a positive objective together, for example, "We need to ensure everybody has the school supplies required at schoolwork time".

. Think of lots of issues. Ensure all players find a workable pace thought for taking care of the problem. At that point, think about the results or outcomes of different decisions. Ask, "What may occur if we attempt…?".

• **GREEN LIGHT** – Go, attempt and reflect.

. Players can run toward you, tap you, and afterward pick an answer or thought most, if not all, preferred. Give it a shot.

. Be sure to ponder it later: "How could it go? Okay, change anything?".

On the off chance that children argue, giving you an inclination word, at that point, offer them alternatives and ask which ones fit their actual feelings. This extends their emotional jargon.

Stage 3. Practice to Grow Skills and Manage Conflict in Healthy Ways.

Your day by day, interactions can be open doors for your child to rehearse new crucial skills if you hold onto those odds. Practice develops imperative new brain associations that fortify (and inevitably structure predispositions) each time your child endeavors to manage sentiments, words, and decisions valuably.

Practice likewise gives significant chances to create considerable reasoning, or the capacity to think ahead to the effect of a specific decision and assess whether it's a favorable decision dependent on those reflections.

Activities.

- Allow your child the opportunity to find a way to address their vast difficulties, assuming liability for their very own connections – in any event, when you realize you could improve.

- Be sure and think about how you can make the conditions to help their prosperity (like contribution instructing or guided open-finished inquiries to incite thinking) with the goal that your child figures out how to turn into their own best issue solver.

- Initially, the practice may require all the more teaching, however, abstain from offering direct arrangements, going legitimately to the next in the conflict, or taking care of an issue for your child.

Stage 4. Bolster Your Child's Development and Success.

Now, you've shown your child how to address their difficulties with ability and determination, and you are enabling them to rehearse so they can figure out how to do those new errands well and autonomously. Presently, you can offer help when it's required by reteaching, observing, instructing, and when suitable, applying practical results. Parents frequently provide support as they see their child fumble with a circumstance wherein they need assistance. This is the same.

By offering help, you are fortifying their capacity to be successful, helping them develop circumstances and logical results thinking (as they address issues and conflicts), and helping them develop skills in assuming liability.

Activities.

- Initially, your child may require dynamic help. Use "Show me" explanations and request that they exhibit how they can operate to determine an issue. At the point when a child learns another ability, they are eager to show it off! You could state, "Show me, you can work out your argument with your sister".

- Recognize effort by utilizing "I notice" explanations like, "I saw how you talked to your sister about how you were feeling and afterward worked with her on an approach to get to an understanding. That is magnificent!"

- On days with additional difficulties when you can see your child is puzzled or feeling inadequate, proactively help your child to remember their quality. In a delicate, non-open way you can murmur in your child's ear, "Remember how you talked to your sister yesterday? You can utilize that same procedure with your companion today".

- Actively think about how your child is feeling when moving toward difficulties. You can pose inquiries like:

  - "How do you feel about your spare time at school?" Offering an opportunity to talk about lunch and break gives an understanding of your child's social difficulties.

  - "It seems like you are holding angry emotions toward your friend. Have you talked to them yet? What choices do you think you have?" Be sure to ponder the results of potential decisions.

- Apply legitimate outcomes when required. Sensible issues should come not long after the negative behavior and should be given in a manner that keeps up a healthy relationship. Instead of discipline, a result is tied in with supporting the learning procedure. To start with, get your feelings within appropriate boundaries. In addition to the fact that this is acceptable, displaying when your emotions are under wraps, you can give intelligent outcomes that fit the behavior. Second, welcome your child into a discourse about the desires built up in Step 2 for overseeing conflict. Third, if you feel that your child isn't holding up their end of the deal (except if it involves them not knowing how), at that point, apply a positive result as a teaching moment.

Try not to proceed onward or bother. Children frequently need more opportunities to manage their emotions and approach somebody with whom they are concerned. Make sure to stand by long enough for your child to come to you if they can address their issues with your help. Your holding up could have a significant effect on whether they can work through their problems.

Stage 5. Perceive Effort and Quality to Foster Motivation.

Even though it is anything but difficult to overlook, your concern is your child's best prize. It's anything but difficult to become involved with the hecticness and business of getting responsibilities achieved in family life. Be that as it may, if your child is trying to work through arguments usefully, it will merit your time and energy to remember it. Your acknowledgment can go far to advancing business as usual positive behaviors and extending your child's feeling of capability and obligation. You can add to your child's inspiration to buckle down by the following activities.

Activities.

- Recognize and respond when it is working out positively. It might appear glaringly evident. However, it's simple not to see when all is moving along smoothly. At the point when your child is boldly confronting their sister who hurt them, for instance, a short, explicit response is much required: "I saw you talked to your sister to attempt to work it out after she hurt you. Indeed! Fantastic".

- Recognize little improvements en route. Try not to sit tight for the enormous achievements – like no family battling – to perceived exertion. Remember that your acknowledgment can fill in as an instrument to advance increasingly positive behaviors. Discover little ways your child is putting forth an attempt and let them realize you see them.

- Build festivities into your daily schedule. For instance, if your child compensates for a poor decision by saying 'sorry' earnestly to a companion, perceive that effort. Incorporate hugs, high fives, and fist bumps in your collection of methods to value each other.

Conflict Coaching and Management For Today's Youth.

Our children are our future. Stop and consider children in the course of the most recent a very long while and how their jobs have changed and advanced throughout the years. How did a child during the 60s or 70s vary from a child during the 80s or 90s? Here we are today, just about ten years into the new thousand years, a period of mind-boggling innovation boosts, the substantial challenge for accomplishment and material increase, changes in sexual orientation jobs and in particular, changes in family elements. Life is ceaselessly changing, and this is normal. We are a consistently developing, regularly evolving society.

In any case, with such sensational moves in social standards and behaviors in the course of the most recent 30 years or something like that, would we be able to in any case hope to bring up and encourage our children as we were instructed when we were youthful, which was predominately in dictator family units? We will take a gander at three individual situations which have been taken from an ongoing family elements study. Each of the three cases is families in the new thousand years raised in the United States.

History has indicated that we frequently don't consider conflict until we need outsiders to help to assist us with sifting through our issues. Directing, intervention, and prosecution are on the whole strategies for conflict resolution. Be that as it may, in the previous decade, more consideration is being put on the brain research perspective conflict by examining family elements, parenting styles, social communications, and conflict resolution education. Before, we have consistently connected questions with a suit, or in the legal sense. Presently, we are taking a gander at conflict and conflict management proactively by endeavoring to comprehend what drives people by and by, and how we can educate society, starting with our children intending to issues in a constructive, beneficial way.

Parental Influence and Behavior.

Here are three cases we can consider. These children are teenagers attempting to endure and discover their way in this day and age. Every child is from another ethnic and strict society, every representative of an exceptional family unit. Add to this the changing parenting styles, social impacts, their foreordained character characteristics, individual

63

objectives, and beneficial experiences, and you can see how every personal methodology conflict alternately.

With all the different impacts on our children today, parents are the #1 impact. We are our children's excellent examples. Parenting styles and their effects on children have been examined throughout the years and have been separated into three classifications: Authoritarian, Permissive, and Authoritative. Understanding the three styles of parenting in connection to conflict resolution is the initial phase in seeing how children think, act, and respond inside their environment.

The Authoritarian Parent. Tyrant parents anticipate that their children should comply with their principles precisely and regularly use prizes and discipline to keep their children in line. With dictator style parenting, a few children endeavor to satisfy their parents to stay away from punishment and don't feel great communicating with the parent their affections because of a paranoid fear of disillusioning their parent or control. A few children may loathe their parents or even renegade against their rigid standards.

The Permissive Parent. This is a lenient type of parenting that gives next to zero structure to the children. No restrictions and rules are regularly made, and if they are, they are incredibly fluffy. Unbounded, children are probably going to make some troublesome memories coexisting with friends and figuring out how to act in the public arena. Lenient parenting is a remarkably free and open type of parenting, one that is often of a single-parent home or a home where the two parents work and don't make family time a need.

The Authoritative Parent. Definitive is a majority rule style of parenting which offsets rights with obligations. This type of parenting enables points of confinement to be set for children while furnishing them with decisions inside those breaking points. By offering choices to your children, you are communicating to them that their assessments are significant, and their choices may convey an undesired result and outcome. Definitive parenting better readies the child for autonomy in the public arena. It gives trains them a bargain and ingrains the understanding that we learn by our decisions and outcomes of those decisions.

Family Dynamics.

Harking back to the '50s and 60's the family unit regularly comprised of the Father/Provider and Mother/Caregiver. The dad was the chief and gave monetarily to the family while the mother dealt with the home and the children. This likewise alludes to the "family unit". During that time, the adjustments in our general public with sexual orientation jobs changing, ladies craving professions outside the home, pushing for correspondence with men, wanting their own money related freedom, and the family unit has changed. Children of separation are more common than any time in recent memory, with the separation rate being at half when contrasted with 22% in 1960. Presently we have an increasingly different family unit made up of single-parent homes, children being raised by grandparents, and mixed families coming about because of remarriage. Tremendous changes in the family center have opened the entryway to numerous other life challenges inside the family unit, particularly relating to the children.

Divorce influences the parent as well as the child too. Studies have indicated that children exhibit their tension over the dissolution of their parents' marriage in changing manners ordinarily dependent upon the age at which the divorce happens. The torment children experience from separation can comprise of helplessness, weakness, distress, misfortune, anger, and feebleness. Also, the connection between the parent and child changes as the custodial parent may experience the disorder, anger, diminished desires for their children for fitting social behavior, or otherwise known as reduced parenting. Besides, studies have indicated that a child's post-separate from personal satisfaction can majorly affect their long-haul change results. Most continuous worries of children are that of rehashing the cycle of a messed-up marriage.

For some parents, life proceeds after separation, and they move onto new connections, which drives them to re-marriage and mixed families. The present commonplace family unit comprises of stepparents, stepchildren, and step-kin. Our children are tossed into "moment" families who have just started to build up their very own arrangement of convictions, norms, ethnic foundations, strict convictions, and parenting styles. New characters, customs, and recollections are altogether added to the mixed family unit. Notwithstanding, a child is as yet the child, and the grown-up is as, however, the grown-up. We should, in any case, recollect that even through the wild changes in the family elements, we should recall that children still need parity of adoration, consideration, and discipline.

Social Influences.

As children develop and go to class, they are profoundly impacted by their friends. They will become pioneers or adherents. They will locate a particular friend group with which they can distinguish and shape fellowships. Friend groups offer children the chance to create different social skills, for example, authority, sharing or cooperation, and sympathy. Friend groups likewise provide the opportunity to try different things with new jobs and collaborations, which is usually the explanation that young people float, starting with one gathering then onto the next as they are in search to "get themselves" or work toward the development of their personality.

Children need acknowledgment, and their friends additionally profoundly impact them. Friend gatherings can have either a negative or a positive impact on a child. At the point when a child needs self-certainty or self-worth, they will go to whatever gatherings that are generally tolerating, paying little heed to the gathering's social and moral behaviors. In any case, peer gatherings can likewise give an effective option to a child that can advance positive practices and advance literary greatness alongside healthy emotional help.

A youngster that has been shown suitable conflict management skills will have a more straightforward opportunity with regards to peer weight and social acknowledgment by figuring out how to adjust the benefit of obliging the group against the significance of settling on their own choices.

Conflict Management and Resolution Styles of Teenagers.

There are three essential methodologies by which teenagers handle conflict: the latent methodology, the forceful methodology, and the emphatic methodology. The method the child takes can hugely affect the result of the difference — the Passive Approach. The inactive process is related to the absence of communication, low self-worth, and dread of the showdown. Aloof children are probably going to be pushed around with next to zero repercussions. Moreover, these children may make some hard memories framing kinships and frequently discover companionships are unfulfilling because of the way that these children are adequately exploited.

The Aggressive Approach. This methodology utilizes terrorizing and confrontation as its essential source settling the conflict. These children will do whatever necessary to arrive at their ideal result, not make any difference in the outcomes. They take a gander at the battle as a success/lose circumstance and think about reactions literally, rather than taking a gander at it as an approach to learn and develop. Forceful children are frequently marked as menaces and are either kept away from or warm up to other comparable children.

The Assertive Approach. A law based style of conflict resolution, children adopt a strategy that joins respect with collaboration and bargain. These children have figured out how to effectively impart to pass on their assessments while contemplating the necessities of others. The emphatic methodology is the best as it can ordinarily bring about a success win answer for all gatherings included. It limits the negative sentiments of anger and disdain likewise with the detached and forceful methodologies and replaces it with positive emotions of self-satisfaction.

Teaching Life Skills.

Teaching our children significant fundamental abilities is essential in helping them with taking care of conflicts as children and conveying these skills into their grown-up years. Up until the previous decade or somewhere in the vicinity, the vast majority of our emphasis has been on conflict resolution for grown-ups. In any case, with the expansion of troublesome behaviors by youths, expanded separation rate, and the communication breakdown among parent and child, experts are currently taking a gander at helping children in finding a progressively profitable approach to deal with conflict. In an ongoing report, sixth and seventh-grade children were examined concerning how boys and girls took care of conflict. Young ladies were found to commonly depend on verbal affirmation, where young men demonstrated progressively forceful inclinations. Self-viability and self-control were seen as critical indicators of conflict resolution styles. Also, it is discovered that by advancing social capabilities in our childhood, psychosocial issues, for example, wrongdoing and medication misuse is diminished, and scholarly accomplishment expanded.

Lately, schools, chapels, and youth programs are executing conflict resolution projects, for example, conflict instructing, conflict management workshops, harmony building workshops, and mediation programs. The proof is demonstrating that by giving our suitable childhood skills at a convenient time, we will encourage them tendencies they can take with them for a lifetime. Teaching the appropriate social and conflict management behaviors has gotten similarly as essential as teaching our children skills in math, science, and social examinations and English. We can never again hold up until we are adults to start to make sense of how to manage conflict. Children will manage conflict from their early stages, so why not build up the suitable skills at a convenient time?

In sports and athletic occasions, we have mentors, and these mentors support and represent athletic skills for the game, advance group play, character, and group solidarity. Throughout everyday life, we need mentors consistently to keep us on track, responsible, to advance cooperation, family solidarity, and show fundamental abilities. Holistic mentors are similarly as crucial for controlling our childhood, as mentors are in directing our group activities. Advisors or guiding is executed to fix something that isn't right. However, we should be taking a gander at behavior from the imminent of encouraging and actualizing the proper skills in our childhood to deal with their everyday conflicts and social issues.

A critical apparatus we have is the web. The introduction of the internet has opened a way to unlimited assets at a bit of a fingertip. Teenagers are one of the most capable of utilizing the web, with 55% of every single online high schooler having at least one social media account. A decent outlet for any high schooler who is confronting an issue and needs to convey their sentiments secretly is by making an online road for teenagers to post their interests and get criticism, without uncovering their characters. A genuine example might be a child being pushed around by a bully. Children don't want to look "weak" or "cowardly," so they don't report or convey when another is badgering them. By having an outlet to talk about and look for help, namelessly keeps the child feeling engaged, and lessens any plausibility of reprisal by the bully.

Our childhood needs outlets for conflict resolution and education and instructing for conflict management. We see development and moderate affirmation of this in the public eye. However, we most become progressively proactive and start concentrating on giving and offering projects to our childhood now. We see an ever-increasing number of issues in our general public, and we need to quit taking a gander at only a fix to the problem. Still, instead, we need to take a gander at proactive approaches to educate and speak with our childhood. It resembles our wellbeing. We can go to the specialist and get a remedy to control hypertension, or we can execute a healthy eating regimen and exercise with an end goal to keep our circulatory strain inside ordinary cutoff points and stay fit.

Tending to conflict with our children has become a significant worry because of our cultural changes over the past couple of decades. As we have seen, there is an assortment of elements that add to how our children handle conflict, parental impact, and social impacts being a substantial factor in a child's view of conflict and how to frame a resolution. All in all, we should quickly take a look at our three cases and check whether we can decide the aspects that add to how these children manage conflict.

As should be obvious, conflict is a piece of life. Regardless of whether we are young or old, there will be issues that need tending to in our marriages, families, organizations, places of worship, schools, and networks. Understanding the brain research of conflict will help us in having the option to all the more likely help our children in building up the skills essential to effectively manage conflict in their lives. Consider how much the world has changed in recent years or thereabouts. Presently attempt to envision the amount more, it will change in the following at least 30 years. Putting resources into conflict resolution instructing and preparing now with our children will assist them with developing the skills that will prompt a progressively beneficial, sure individual later on.

CHAPTER FIVE

HOW TO TEACH CHILDREN SELF-RESPECT.

There is a saying that goes something like this: "respect isn't merited until it is earned". Concerning teaching, children respect, activities talk stronger than words. You can say quite a few things to your child about having respect for other people be that as it may until you have demonstrated compliance, it will no doubt fail to attract anyone's attention. That stated, unmistakably, parents have an enormous obligation at both appearing and teaching respect to their children and, in this manner, empower their children to shape healthy respect for other people.

As has just been brought up, the best method for teaching your children the craft of respect is to show it through your very own activities. At the point when you clarify the significance of saying 'please' and 'thank you' by doing it without anyone's help, you strengthen in your children how they ought to likewise act. An ideal application is to request your children's assistance around the house and, when they complete the errand, express gratitude toward them. Give them praise for work very much done; this will impart in them the craving to show excellent behavior since it will assist them with feeling great about what they have done to help other people.

Children that are balanced at home and have a solid feeling of self-worth are socially capable out in the open and will reflect your great habits to other people. When a child likes themselves, they are bound to approach others with respect and appreciation.

As their parents, you will do well by your children by urging them to offer demonstrations of benevolence and liberality to others by indicating respect. A soul of collaboration is a lovely thing and increased in value by others. At the point when they are more youthful, let them realize that the proper activity is different. Regardless of whether it is with a toy or on the swing, when they finish your teaching on appropriate respect for other people, praise them liberally. Try to disclose to them how pleased you are of them for being amenable and respectful of others.

One last idea: children usually comprehend what it is to be harmed by the heartless demonstrations of others, yet they don't often have the foggiest idea of how to react to this emotional damage they experienced appropriately. It is your obligation as their parents to pass on why others hurt and afterward to encourage them not to hurt back. To return, fiendish for underhanded is never the appropriate response. To return useful for cruel is an unusual way to deal with figuring out how to deal with all circumstances, both great and terrible. This kind of reaction is born from somebody who isn't just OK with what their identity is, yet has been instructed poorly on how to show respect in a world that can be pitiless. You will do well as parents to pass on this mentality in your children to not just protect their hearts should somebody strikeout frightfully, however, to likewise set them up to go out and improve the world by first respecting themselves.

Show Children Respect.

Teaching children about respecting others originates from talking to them about it as well as demonstrating them. If you get them to become familiar with this important exercise, you will have to approach your child with respect and nobility. Children learn by viewing. If they see you approaching others with respect, chances are they will stick to this same pattern. You can show your children how to have healthy connections with how you treat your loved ones.

Children model behavior they find in grown-ups. Regardless of whether it is their parents, a teacher, or other noteworthy grown-up children are continually watching and learning. In school, it is especially significant for their instructors to treat their peers well. Considering the amount of tormenting that goes on in schools today, their educators affect the standard of respect the children should take one another. On the off chance that an instructor is especially brutal or ill-intended to anyone student, different students will consider this to be permitted for them likewise to treat that child inadequately. Being children, they believe that what grown-ups do is the right method for carrying on, not understanding that the instructor is likewise a bully.

Children realize how harmful ridiculing or tormenting can be and how it affects them. They need to be dealt with genuinely, like all of us. They may not realize how to treat individuals, so as a parent, you should show them the way. Show your child how to play decently, and they will give this knowledge to their friends. Some portion of respecting someone else is showing resistance. This implies tolerating them for what their identity is, the things that they wear, where they live, or who their parents are just as the religion they follow or nation of cause.

A little respect goes far. What number of differences could be settled with a bit of respect? What number of wars would not host been battled had each get-together respected the other's supposition or convictions? Teaching your child to be courteous and kind will go far to having them grow up to be healthy and contributing grown-ups. As a parent, you commit to showing them the way. At the point when you offer assistance to others, you are telling your children the best way to act. Adulating your child for a vacation all around done or for good behavior is another approach to impart respect and reverence in your child.

Not exclusively will they like themselves, yet you will love the sort of individual you are raising, and having children who grow up to be socially capable, who have a solid feeling of self-esteem and approach individuals with respect, ought to be worth it. Our children are what is to come. By giving them the devices that they will require as grown-ups, we set our children up to be useful, beneficial, and happy.

Parenting Discipline - Teaching Children Self Respect, Self-Control, and Empathy.

For some parents, the words "parenting discipline" have extremely negative undertones. There is the relationship with their childhood and the frequently unsavory memories. At that point, there is a relationship with the word discipline with thoughts around beating, punishing, hitting, and harming children. A few parents accept that the names "parenting discipline" and their concept of bringing up children ought not to be referenced in a similar sentence. To them, it feels cruel and sounds reformatory. They might instead want to consider theories of loving prizes, kind words, and respectful limits.

Parenting discipline, for me, is tied in with teaching children methods to develop that empower them to be protected, have self-respect, self-control, and compassion for other people. Our children need us to give them how, and they learn by demonstrating their behavior on our own. For me, great discipline is tied in with being firm, transparent, and predictable as parents - about being positive, kind, and respectful - about appearing, teaching, and empowering our children. I don't have confidence in unforgiving, corrective, or rebuffing strategies for discipline. However, I am a firm adherent that all children need to have limits and breaking points, and they need us to set up these cutoff points for them. I accept that at the core of good parenting discipline are clarifications, discussions, teaching, and results.

Teaching through Understanding.

Since the beginning, our children need our endorsement. They have to realize that they are adored, loved, and needed. They genuinely don't prefer to be unwell with us and would, in every case, instead feel firmly appended. As it were, they need to make the right decision to have steady support. They need to realize how to make the best decision, and they need us to show them the approach to this.

By disclosing and helping them to comprehend, our children can figure out how to make the best choice. This technique for discipline functions admirably when a customary spot in the house is utilized as the 'teaching and clarifying' place. Perhaps you will decide to sit in a similar spot in the lounge room each time you clarify what behavior is required. I would, in general, sit my children up on a high bar stool at the kitchen seat so I could keep in touch with them more easily.

Request that your child mentions to you what occurred.

"I dropped food on the rug".

At that point, ask as to for what reason do you believe that occurred?

"I was sitting in front of the TV".

What would you be able to do any other way next time?

"Sit at the table".

How might we fix this?

"I can clean it up".

Right, please do that now.

Indeed, even small kids can adapt better if there is a ramification for their behavior. For this situation, tidying up and turning off the TV was the outcome. There is no discipline going on here, merely personal outcomes for their activities. This all requires some serious energy, consideration, and vitality and necessitates that you are in a quiet and thoughtful spot with your child. If the behavior is far worse than dropping food, for example, you may need to demand a break until you quiet down. Your teaching discussion should be age-suitable and changed following your children's capacity. The magnificence of this technique is that children figure out how to consider their behavior, its outcomes consequences for other people, and how to settle on changes and decisions.

Parenting Discipline through Boundaries and Limits.

Children adapt best when rules are primarily and unmistakably expressed. As they develop and create, you can enable your children to set their very own limits and to choose what their significant limits are by continually expanding their chances of settling on their own choices. As you watch children's creating awareness of other's expectations, they flourish with rules and points of confinement. Tune in to any gathering of children playing, and it turns out to be evident that they set the standards for their games plainly and with a definite purpose. They like to realize what is relied upon and how to go about it.

Setting the essential points of confinement and positively characterizing them causes children to turn out to be acceptable leaders. For example, rather than saying, "Buckle your seatbelt," try clarifying that the vehicle doesn't move until all safety belts are buckled up! Rather than saying, "Don't drop your food on the carpet," try saying, we as a whole eat best when sitting up to the table. Defining limits isn't tied in with policing your children, it's tied in with teaching them to respect the rights and needs of others just as themselves.

Parenting Discipline through Consequences.

More established children adapt rapidly on the off chance that they experience the results of their negative behavior. They can quickly comprehend circumstances and logical consequences and figure out how to have an awareness of other's expectations. Encountering outcomes additionally encourages children to turn out to be progressively sympathetic and mindful of their environment. Every one of our activities affects one way or another or other on the planet and children who grow up knowing this become increasingly cautious, kind-hearted, and empathetic. I accept that encountering the results of their own adverse decisions shows children more rapidly than some other 'restraining' strategy. Children who are instructed how to think, how to think about others, and how to assume liability for their behavior become roused, natural, unconstrained, and imaginative people.

They become anxious for information, build up a solid feeling of moral duty, and figure out how to be tolerant, warm, and minding people. Regular, sensible outcomes are a child's best instructor. For example, on the off chance that you don't wear a coat, you get cold and wet. On the off chance that you overlook your game jersey, you can't partake. On the off chance that you don't pack your lunch, you will be hungry. If you break or damage something through your thoughtlessness, you should replace it. Parenting discipline is tied in with teaching your children with empathy and concerning being as well as can be expected - to have an independent mind, to experience the outcomes of their behavior, and to assume liability for their action. The prizes are warm, compassionate, accommodating, mindful people who show mindfulness for themselves, their environment, and for one another.

CHAPTER SIX

MOVING WITH YOUR CHILDREN.

When To Discuss The Move.

When you have definite plans, you should tell the older children. They need a lot of time to work things through and make their very own changes. Bidding farewell to friends can't be rushed. By hiding your move until the latest possible time, you run the hazard that they will catch wind of it from another person, and this could be shocking to them.

More Youthful Children.

It is better NOT to tell little youngsters that you are moving until movement is in progress, which includes them. A small child can't completely comprehend what a movie is about. The more they need to envision things in their brains, the more apprehensive and startled they may become.

Step by Step Instructions to Discuss The Move.

Most importantly, your state of mind will hugely affect your child. On the off chance that your frame of mind is one of experience, and if you remain concentrated on the positive changes the move will make, this will channel down to your children and help them mentally prepare following the progress. Then again, if you are focused, stressed, or discouraged, your child will pick up on this additionally and potentially respond negatively. There is no more significant dread than the dread of the unknown. Accordingly, give the same number of insights regarding the transition to your child as you feel is vital. Children need to know why the family is moving and what will occur during the move. Consistently, stay perky and energized, especially on the off chance that you are talking about the new home and neighborhood.

You should hold customary "Moving Talks" with the remainder of the family. As of now, encourage your children to ask questions and voice their feelings. Practically all children have a change in security from a disruption of this magnitude. Listen mindfully, respect their issues, and address their interests lovingly and importantly.

Particularly For Small Children.

A small kid will be centered around the present. Along these lines, the idea of moving in half a month (not to mention months) won't mean a lot to them. They will be promptly rushing to the window, searching for the moving van, and turning out to be baffled when it isn't there yet. Furthermore, little children retain information through dreams and playing. Take a stab at utilizing boxes and a wagon to assist them with understanding the idea of moving. Have your child cautiously load up the cart and afterward have that person bring the wagon into another space to empty the substance.

You can likewise acquaint your little children with moving by giving those picture books of other children moving. Ensure you see how the individuals in the book may be feeling. (Regardless of what the story, consistently ensure that you end up on a bright and happy note).

Potential Reactions To The Move:

As a parent, you must stay mindful of your children's dispositions during this disrupting time. On the off chance that a child isn't responding as you would have expected (for example, uncommonly impartial or exhausted), at that point, it may be a sign of some significant inside issues at work. Help them to bring their valid feelings out away from any visible impediment. Promise them that it is alright to differ with you. When the issues are on the table, at that point, an answer can be worked out. ALL children are going to give some level of dissatisfaction, anger, apprehension, and bitterness through the span of the move ...and for a couple of months after subsiding into your new home.

Abstain from getting heated with your adolescent. They will defy sayings, for example, 'there is no reason to worry.' Instead, be open, legit, and respective towards their interests. Tell them that you need to help discover answers for any issues, and afterward ensure that you finish any guarantee. Try not to guarantee whatever you can't convey. This is an opportunity to create trust and a bond. Keep them legitimately in the "moving picture". Look for their recommendation and give them a specific degree of obligation and essential leadership. Tell them that they are significant and that you need their info and input.

Presenting Your New Home: Arrange A Sneak Preview.

Preferably, you should design a visit to the new home with your children before moving. This visit will offer structure to the progress and cause it to appear to be all the more genuine. If the house is unfilled, head inside and let your family check out their rooms. Invest some energy mapping out where the furniture will be going. Acquaint yourself with any families in the area. Look at the cafés, motion picture films, sports offices, parks, play areas, shops, and so forth. If practical, sign your children up for any additional exercises, while they are with you. Along these lines, they will see the offices, meet the individuals, and it won't seem so odd and frightening later. Conceivably orchestrate a speedy voyage through the school(s) your children will visit. On the off chance that you realize who will show your child, presently would be an incredible time to acclimate.

If Your Child Can't Go With You,

If your new home is excessively far away for visits, at that point, it becomes significant that you either photo it or tape it for your children when you are there. Take the perspectives out the windows and incorporate the front and back yard. Remember to record different destinations of intrigue (schools, shops, eateries, parks, sports fields, play areas, and so on). Take pictures of other children at a similar age to your family. Your very own children will need to perceive what they are wearing, regardless of whether they look neighborly, and where they are hanging out. Afterward, take pictures as a guide of the area, so your child can get some feeling of spatial separations. Make up singular "Care Packs" with blessing confirmations or coupons to attractions and cafés that they would each discover energizing. Incorporate a unique token from one of the new shops. Tell them what bus stations are accessible, what music stations kids are listening to, and what motion pictures are at present appearing. Develop energy and enthusiasm.

Include Your Children: Create A Sense Of Teamwork.

Giving your children age-explicit occupations will assist them with feeling included. For example, your rudimentary age child may cherish making records and ticking off occupations as they are finished, while your teenager can accept accountability in arranging of furniture. Ensure you accentuate how much their help is valued. Encourage your family to advance their concerns regarding various parts of the move. Outline every child's room, with their furniture piece to scale, and enable them to begin orchestrating things. Let your children choose their paint hues, and ensure you at that point take them with you when looking for any room beautifying something, for example, paint, backdrop, quilts, and so on. This can be an energizing and sensational experience and gives your child a feeling of improving.

Include your children with packing their things in their rooms. More seasoned children can pack every one of their effects, while a more youthful child ought to be encouraged to pack one box with extraordinary toys. (On the off chance that your little child is stressed over the toy vanishing, put it aside where it can, without much of a stretch be seen, and afterward take it with you in the vehicle on moving day). Orchestrate every child to customize the outside of their box by providing stickers or shaded pens. Request that the movers load these containers last, with the goal that they will be the leading when the moving van lands at your new home.

Making Life Easier: Avoid Unnecessary Change.

Attempt to keep away from any movements to your child's day by day schedule. Typical nap times, playtimes, dinner times, and sleep times ought to be kept up, and any extra charges (for example, potty training) ought to be put on hold until a little while after you have moved into your new house. If you have certain family customs (for example, Friday night pizzas), ensure that you still respect them. Moving is such a significant change for a child. Try not to include different modifications on top of it. Children will require the steadiness of regular routines. Even though this appears as though a smart thought to toss out your child's old toys and garments, it is better that you cling to them until after the move.

Every one of these items, regardless of how worn and worn out, can help make the change from the known into the obscure much more straightforward for children. If conceivable, pack your child's room last. This is their private space and a unique spot to go when things get overwhelming. Try not to pack most loved items or dress into boxes for the moving van. Instead, take them with you in the vehicle (if conceivable), so they will never be excessively far away. On the off chance that it is plausible when it comes time to pack your little child's room, do as such while they are in childcare or out of the house, visiting a neighbor. That way, they aren't a piece of the last change, and you can give them a great deal of attention when they return.

Bidding farewell:

Farewell To the House.

There are a ton of recollections in your home. This remains constant for your children just as for yourself. You may wish to think about taking loads of photos before you start to disassemble and pack. Have your child make a "Memory Book" and fill it with pictures of the spots and individuals in your local that have implied a great deal to the person in question.

Farewell to Friends.

Bidding farewell to companions and friends and family will be the most emotional piece of any move. Older children can hold a get-together. As of now, they can give out postcards previously stamped and addressed with their new location (nothing like getting a downpour of mail directly after the move), have everybody record their contact information and individual note in a collection and ensure you film the gathering or at least take heaps of photographs. In the wake of settling into your new home, ensure you give your children loads of opportunities to stay in contact with their old companions. Maybe even give them an extraordinary extended goodbye phone allowance. Organize past friends to come and visit, or even calendar an arrival visit to your new neighborhood once in a while.

Moving Day:

Newborn children and little children are vastly improved off remaining with grandparents, aunties or uncles. This will help cause the change to go all the more easily and keep away from any mischief coming to them from disrupting the general flow. They will likewise be confounded concerning why you can't give them their ordinary degree of attention and could wind up feeling left out. On the off chance that this is absurd, at that point, protect newborn children in a playpen alongside their most loved toys and consider hiring a more seasoned, dependable neighbor to come and play with your more youthful children and to watch out for everybody.

Try not to pack your child's most loved toys and books in moving boxes. Rather keep these treasures with you so they will be effectively open when you land at the new home. Likewise, keep out certain games for the vehicle, in case weariness sets in. Plan to park in front of the movers. This enables time for your children to investigate before the rooms are covered in boxes. Ensure you give your child heaps of jobs to do as the furnishings and boxes are unpacked. Everything will appear to be abnormal, and it assists with focusing on something explicit, as opposed to allowing the psyche to mind.

Make sure to attempt to stay as positive and as quiet as conceivable on this day. Your children will be looking to you for comfort. Lots of hugs and grins will go far.

Settling In:

Upon appearance, deal with your child's room first. This will offer them a sentiment of security and go about as a base. Immediately set up their furnishings and enable your children to unload their containers. Encourage them to organize specific things about how they feel is generally satisfying. Next, check the homesite for anything that may cause a potential mishap (shaky railings and steps, free window screens, opened entryways, unprotected pools, and so on).. At that point, build up physical limits with your children. Tell them the regions that they are permitted to investigate without anyone else.

Try not to attempt to unload everything simultaneously. When the basic things have been uncovered, take a few "Disclosure Breaks". Take short strolls through the new neighborhood, or jump in the vehicle and look at the nearest eatery or park. Investigate exercises going on at the neighborhood library. Maybe your new town has a gallery or zoo, or on the other hand a bicycle ride. Set aside an effort to appreciate and assimilate the environment. Unload progressively.

As quickly as time permits, sign your children up for similar exercises they had recently been engaged with (artistry, performing, sports, swimming, and so on).. This will give a sentiment of congruity and help them to meet others with comparable interests. Welcome any local children over for pizza or a grill.

Acclimating to The Change: What To Expect.

When the energy of the move has worn off, and you have sunk into the new house, reality will soak in for children. This is when dissatisfaction and anger may surface as they usually think about what they left behind (home, companions, school, and occupation) with what they presently need to set up. Every child will change unexpectedly. Some will fit in immediately. For other people, it may take significantly longer for the new network to try and start to contrast and the past one. This time of change can take anyplace from half a month to over a year.

Cautioning Signs.

Even though the response to a move is typical, parents should search for signs that show that your child is having a bizarre measure of trouble in changing following the new environment. These admonition signs can include:

- Becoming increasingly pulled back.

- Having trouble sleeping or having bad dreams.

- Excessive crying.

- Excessive upheavals of anger.

- Not having any desire to associate with other children.

- Depression.

- Wanting to be separated from everyone else.

- Headaches/stomachaches.

- Thumb Sucking/bedwetting.

- Lack of craving.

- Lower grades in school.

On the off chance that these side effects continue over a significant period, or if the manifestations are getting worse, at that point, parents should look for guidance from their family specialist or pediatrician.

CHAPTER SEVEN

HOW TO MAKE YOUR CHILD RESPECT OTHERS.

The respectful child: How to show respect (ages 6 to 8).

Show respectful behavior. We don't, for the most part, give our children the sort of respect that we request from them. We forget because frequently, our childhood causes us to compare compliance with dread: 'I truly respected my dad since I realized he'd hit me if ... ' that is not respect — that is dread. Instead, start by listening. In day by day discussion, look at your child without flinching and clarify that you're keen on what she's saying. To attend all the more officially, hold regular family gatherings where everybody — including your evaluation schooler — can air their thoughts and conclusions about issues confronting the entire family.

Show affable reactions. Your adolescent can show thinking about others through great habits. By this age, she should state "please" and "thank you" regularly and need only the occasional reminder. Clarify that you'd preferably help her when she's gracious to you and that you don't care for it when she bosses you around. Once more, being respectful yourself works more effectively. State "please" and "thank you" to your child (and others), and she'll discover that the expressions are a piece of ordinary communication, both inside your family and out in the open.

Abstain from overcompensating. If your middle schooler considers you a "butthead," do whatever it takes not to get annoyed (hello, in any event, you don't have cooties!). A child who needs to incite a response will suffer practically any obnoxiousness just to aggravate you. Instead, get eye to eye and state discreetly yet immovably, "We don't call each other names in this family". Then tell her the best way to get what she needs respectfully: "When you need me to support you, simply ask me, please. Say, 'Mother, I need some help with my art project please.'"

Anticipate contradictions. Life would be a lot simpler if our children in every case cheerfully consented to our requests. However, that is not sensible. Attempt to recall that when your middle schooler doesn't take your offering, she isn't attempting to be disrespectful — she simply has an alternate conclusion. Instruct her that she'll fare better on the off chance that she can figure out how to quit conveying everything that needs to be said disrespectfully ("You never take me for bicycle rides, and I hate you!") and instead figure out how to put a definite turn on her solicitations ("Can we please go bicycle riding after the grocery store?").

Set points of confinement. Probably the ideal approach to show respect is to be both kind and firm in the entirety of your discipline. Being caring shows respect for your child, and being firm demonstrates respect for what should be finished. So if your middle schooler has a tantrum in the clothing store and none of your adapting strategies work, what do you do? On the off chance that the shopping can be delayed, say to her unassumingly, "We're going to leave now and return to the store some other time when you're feeling quieter. On the off chance that the task needs to complete, walk a couple of feet from your child in the wake of informing her, "I'll be directly here where you can see me. Tell me when you're feeling quieter, and afterward, we can wrap up our shopping". If the emergency proceeds, you can generally lead your child out to the vehicle, where she can gather herself in private.

Talk it over later. Some of the time, the ideal approach to deal with disrespect is to talk about it with your middle schooler then, whenever you've both got an opportunity to relax. You can acknowledge her emotions and come to your meaningful conclusion by saying, "Honey, I could tell you were especially frustrated. What do you think caused that? What thoughts do you need to take care of the issue? What might be a more respectful way to let me know how you're feeling?" One error parents make is that they attempt to force outcomes as opposed to helping children investigate results. On the off chance that your child accepts that you're incredibly interested in her reasoning, she'll regularly reach a similar resolution that you would.

Acclaim respectful behavior. Strengthen your middle schooler's impromptu acts of flexibility, however much as could be expected. Be that as it may, be explicit. "The recognition ought to depict the behavior in detail. We will work in generalities, say, 'I'm pleased with you,' or 'great job. Instead, state, "Thank you for saying please when you requested a snack," or "Thank you for asking my permission before you took the scissors from my work area". Be explicit, and your child will rapidly discover that her endeavors are advantageous and acknowledged.

Youngsters: How to Get Your Child to Listen.

Numerous parents today are baffled and left scratching their heads while attempting to make sense of how to get their high schoolers to hear them out. With so much information and advice available, they are left baffled as a substantial part of the information neglects to work or work conflictingly. One of the most troubling things to change is "close to home" behavior. This behavior makes it significantly more and more troublesome, on the off chance that you are attempting to change the tone of your uncooperative kids, more explicitly, your children's listening tendencies. As you may have just made sense of, be that as it may, is that you can't make your kids change on the off chance that they would prefer not to. No measure of arguing, constraining, or rebuffing will work. The more you demand, the more they will revolt (if not right away then in the end).

The inquiry is, how might you make your child WANT to change his/her demeanor towards listening to you? The appropriate response is to inspect the nature of the connection between you and your child. A useful link is fundamental to a decent relationship, so they will WANT to hear you out (remember, you can't make them!). Connection implies bond. What sort of band do you have with your high schooler? One suggestion to the quality of your high schooler's relationship to you is by how willing s/he is to collaborate. At the point when your child frames a healthy connection to you, everything else will flow smoother.

Note that the connection I am alluding to is the emotional association between the parent and child. This is not quite the same as your child being monetarily subject to you (or relying upon you for vehicle rides). It is an emotional connection you need to make. On the off chance that you make a powerful emotional connection with your child, you will see an expansion in respect, listening, participation, and a generally positive change in his/her frame of mind.

How might you manufacture your connection with your child? Here are five hints you can join into your day by day parenting life.

1. Consistency: Most individuals think flexibility implies approving what you state each time a child disrupts norms. That isn't what I mean for this situation. Consistency suggests that everyday activities coordinate the value ethic you lecture your kids. Your kids will be less disposed to build a loving relationship with you on the off chance that you are excluded from the very principles they need to follow. On the off chance that your behavior is conflicting with your words, you will be seen as a wolf in sheep's clothing, and your high schooler will get companions who keep the same standards from them.

2. Impart: Sit down with your adolescent and examine what is at the forefront of your thoughts. This incorporates making arrangements together, sharing triumphs, sharing great memories, enjoyment past experiences, and jokes. As of late specialists have been concentrating on the significance of communication when things turn out badly. We should not overlook, be that as it may, how important communication is when things are going RIGHT. By communicating the beneficial things, we are strengthening our association with our kids and maintaining their emphasis on us.

3. Association: Decide to be at the table for a couple of moments (15 least!) while your high schooler is examining the day or doing work. Stop what you are doing and commit your whole spotlight on him/

her. It's increasingly amusing to talk when we realize we are tuned in. Eye to eye connection grins and open body language offers more than talking to your teenager while you are hurrying around the kitchen to complete an errand. Effectively tune in to what you are being told. In like manner, share what is on your agenda and examine a portion of your musings and sentiments. These basic motions will show your high schooler s/he matters to you. At the point when you share s/he will share. This kind of contribution to your child's life will push them to hear you out and coordinate.

4. Quality time: Quality time is significant, and it is not the same as filling each other in on what occurred during the day. This is the time you spend together and cause the remainder of the world to vanish. On the off chance that you choose to go out to see the films, line it up with hot cocoa, so despite everything, you have that opportunity to communicate and bond. Communication is the way to building connections since it offers your child a chance to share data about oneself. Opening up and sharing individual data strengthens your child's emotional bond with you.

5. Dependability: Your teenager may frequently say to you that you are never on his/her side. Furthermore, even though I am not urging you to agree with them, but on the off chance that they are off base, in any event, let them have their state. Try not to frame a feeling until you have heard proof from all sides, and you can disclose to your youngster how you formed your verdict. If s/he is genuinely off base, it isn't the issue. Remain active and ask how you can help next time so s/he can settle on better-shaped choices. By offering authenticity, s/he has the motivation to stay by you next time.

The most effective method to Raise Your Child's Self-Esteem.

What number of parents couldn't care less about their child's capacity to succeed and exceed expectations throughout everyday life? Not very many, I think. Is it safe to say that it isn't our objective as parents to raise our child with the qualities, convictions, and self-esteem they need to empower them to address life's difficulties effectively and with certainty? However, what number of parents stress that their child might not have the skills and devices essential to achieve these objectives?

These parents feel that they are doing as well as can be expected; however, stress that there is as yet something incorrect that should be fixed with the goal that their child will have higher self-esteem. It is thus that I give you some practical recommendations that you can do right now to help improve your child's self-esteem. It is never past the point where it is possible to encourage and engage your child!

High self-esteem is created when a child feels that he has a significant place in the world. He has a feeling of feeling vital, acknowledged, and esteemed. At the point when the child grows up feeling cute and fit; he grows high self-esteem. If he is glad for his achievements, he accepts accountability and is responsible for his activities. He can endure dissatisfaction, have the courage to attempt new things, considers setbacks to be difficult, and has sympathy and compassion for other people. To impact a child to have this self-esteem, the parents should have the option to an excellent example of these characteristics also. While none of us are substantial and we as a whole do as well as can be expected, parents are the essential influencer of how their child sees the world and himself.

You are probably not going to discover a child with high self-esteem, originating from parents who are directive, furious, or eager. This sort of environment will, in general, produce children with nervousness, frailty, and self-question. When you have a parent who has not learned the skills to manage their dissatisfaction, disillusionment, and anxiety, for what reason would you be astonished to discover a child who is inadequate with regards to these equivalent skills?

To have high self-esteem, the child needs to feel they are protected to commit errors and not feel disparaged or dishonorable. It is not necessarily the case that the parent ought not to set breaking points or give consequences for inappropriate or harmful behaviors. That is a parent's obligation. It is, notwithstanding, the way wherein these messages are passed on that directs whether the child feels remedied or dismissed. Most parents would prefer not deliberately to hurt their children. However, few have the communication skills to have the option to "parent" without being impacted by their sentiments of need, dissatisfaction, or disillusionment. These qualities and attitudes are what the child hears and means imply that he has fizzled, and this message can have an additionally destroying impact on the child's self-esteem than whatever issues were being tended to.

Every child needs to locate his place in the family and on the planet. He needs to feel that he is novel and extraordinary somehow or another. He needs to discover leisure activities, creates skills or interests that cause him to feel glad and achieved. Parents can encourage this uniqueness by helping the child to investigate different rewards, abilities, or side interests that the child may appreciate.

Tips for building your child's self-esteem.

1. Encourage your child to put forth a valiant effort without expecting perfection. We as a whole commit errors; all children need to feel that it is protected to commit the mistakes without feeling they frustrated their parents. Desires should be sensible, dependent on the child's age and experience.

2. Be reliable. Characterize cutoff points and rules unmistakably. Try not to make guarantees you can't keep or give results that you can't or won't finish. If your child can't confide in your promise, at that point, he will lose respect for you and quit telling in you.

3. Become mindful of what you state and how you assert it. Talk about issues without putting fault. Children remember what you say about yourself as well as other people, and they may repeat similar negatives and reactions to themselves about themselves. It is significantly harder for a child to keep up healthy self-esteem if he feels his parents don't esteem and respect themselves.

4. Be the model you need to set. Try not to advise your child to quit annoying or harassing his sister, if your partner is doing likewise to you.

5. Show your child fondness and reveal to him you love them. Something children have requested when questioned concerning what they are absent from their parents, was to be told they are cherished. You may accept that your child knows this from every one of the things you get him or spots you take him. However, your child needs to hear it also.

6. Give your child a responsibility. He has to realize that he is a significant piece of the family, and like this has specific duties. It will cause your child to feel more put resources into the family if there are desires and responsibilities.

7. Get some information about their feelings. Encourage him to make changes. Get some information about his day. How is school? How are the instructors treating you? Do you have somebody to have lunch with? These inquiries will assist you in finding how your child truly is getting along at school. Try not to expect he will let you know whether he is unhappy or somebody has offended him. Most children don't understand these sentiments. They figure their parents won't have the option to help them at any rate.

8. Try not to contrast one family member with another. Every child is extraordinary and has his very own one-of-a-kind character. It's alright to anticipate that specific behaviors and rules should be respected, yet contrasting one child with another solitary breeds disdain and discouragement, it doesn't motivate.

9. Approach your child with respect. Try not to intrude on him when he is talking, listen mindfully, and give him eye to eye connection. On the off chance that you need him to approach you and others with respect, you should demonstrate similar behaviors.

10. Give every child some alone time with you. It tends to be only 15 or 20 minutes, however playing a game with them, or perusing them a story or merely listening to them talk about what intrigues them, will be respected by your child and help them to feel unique, admirable, and significant. Isn't that how we as a whole need our children to feel?

Approaches to Handle Disrespectful Behavior From Children.

Regardless of whether your child feigns exacerbation and says, "Whatever Mom!" when you advise her to begin her schoolwork, or she imagines she can't hear you when you encourage her to finish her homework, is on the gentle finish of the disrespect range. On the more natural finish of the disrespectful behavior range, you'll discover behaviors, for example, calling individuals names, dismissing the standards, or real animosity. Regardless of where your child falls on the range, it's critical to address disrespect before it deteriorates. An examination found that disrespectful children are probably going to become inconsiderate grown-ups. So while you may be enticed to pardon insolence by making statements like, "Well kids can't avoid being kids," forgetting about it won't help your child. Kids need to figure out how to approach others with respect so they can create strong associations with peers, authority figures, and family individuals.

Your child's disrespect might be a sign he needs assistance in adapting socially suitable approaches to manage his anger, manage disappointment, and impart effectively. Here are the best ramifications for disrespectful behavior:

1. Disregard Attention Seeking Behavior.

It might appear overlooking minor disrespect is equivalent to enabling your child to pull off it. However, particular overlooking can be one of the best adverse outcomes. Overlooking doesn't mean letting your child pull off being mean, in any case. Instead, it's tied in with declining to make your child's disrespect wreck you from the job that needs to be done. On the off chance that you advise your child to clean up his room, and he gets frustrated, don't engage in a prolonged dispute over his disrespectful behavior. Every moment you spend in a force battle is more time than he'll put off tidying up his room. Give him a warning about what will occur on the off chance that he doesn't find a workable pace.

If eye-rolling has become a typical issue, address the issue sometime in the not too distant future when both of you are quiet. State something like, "Prior today when I asked you to tidy up your room, you acted rudely. Do you know that you do that when you're annoyed?" Talk about the potential outcomes of disrespect. Ask, "Do you imagine that you roll your eyes when your companion says something you don't care for?" Engage in a talk about how others feel when they witness impolite behavior. Clarify the regular ramifications for disrespectful behavior, for example, "Disrespectful children frequently experience difficulty making friends".

2. Grandmother's Rule of Discipline.

Grandmother's standard of discipline is a straightforward, however practical approach to get your child to agree. Rather than mentioning to your child what he can't do, reveal to him how he can get help. So instead of saying, "If you don't get it now, you won't have the option to play outside," state, "You can play outside when you are done picking up your toys". Then, leave and surrender it over to your child to get a hold of himself. You additionally may have a go at making statements like, "When you bring down your voice and talk serenely, I'll answer you," or "I'll play with you when you quit being bossy". Teach your child that courteous and kind behavior yields positive outcomes.

3. Give a Single Warning.

Utilize an "assuming... at that point," articulation to caution your child what will occur if the behavior doesn't change. State, "If you don't want quit impeding when I'm on the telephone, at that point, you'll have to go to your room". This offers your child a chance to change his behavior around. Simply ensure you're prepared to finish a negative result if he doesn't agree. Abstain from rehashing your warnings again and again. Else, you'll be preparing your child not to tune in.

4. Give a Negative Consequence.

Most disrespectful behaviors should bring about a quick negative result. Take your child's age and the earnestness of the offense into thought while deciding discipline. The timeout can be a valid negative ramification for small kids. If your 6-year-old yells at you when he's furious, for instance, send him to timeout. Consistent results can be useful for more established children and youngsters. On the off chance that your high schooler exits the entryway after you've disclosed to him, that he can't leave, or your child calls you a name, remove his benefits. You may take his phone for 24 hours or ground him from going out for two days.

5. Use Restitution.

On the off chance that your child or high schooler acts disrespectfully, compensation might be essential to discourage it from happening once more. Compensation is tied in with accomplishing something kind for the person in question or planning something to make reparations for the damage that has been finished. If your child hits her sibling, cause her to do her sibling's tasks for the afternoon. Or on the other hand, if your adolescent breaks something out of anger, make her fix it or pay to get it fixed. Show your child that platitude, "I'm sad," doesn't generally fix things. Compensation will assist her with assuming liability for her disrespectful behavior while additionally attempting to fix the relationship.

At the point when you're tending to disrespectful behavior, its typical for your child to make two stages forward and one strides back. So while he might be courteous and kind one day, he may battle the following. Predictable discipline is the way to helping him gain ground over the long haul. Point out his exemplary behavior when you see it. Also, when he's having a terrible day, consider his disrespect as a sign that he needs more practice. Above all, be a decent good example. Regardless of whether you're baffled with the service you get at an eatery, or you're angry at the telemarketer who intruded on your supper, approach others with respect, and your child will take action accordingly.

CHAPTER EIGHT

FOSTERING A LOVING FAMILY CULTURE.

With the present society advancing immediate satisfaction, accommodation, excitement, and the amassing of "stuff," it's very nearly a given that our children will wind up embracing these equivalent qualities. We, as a whole, observe more youthful kids strolling around with a type of gadget in their hand, iPads, computer games, and such. Even though that in itself isn't an issue, it is the de-accentuation of childhood and family that is the more significant concern. We have to perceive the effect our culture is having on our children as people and our families.

How would we take on this conflict with society? Where do we start? First, beginning by asking yourselves these significant inquiries: What do we need for our family? What are our qualities, convictions, and objectives? Am I not catching it means to be an individual from our family?

Next, set aside the effort to talk about these with your partner and offer with your children in age-proper ways. Have a Family Night that incorporates some talk time. Do this toward the start, enduring around 5-15 minutes relying upon your kids' ages. Impart your desires obviously and definitely. For instance, "The Smith's practice good eating habits". rather than saying, "No more fast food". Create the illustrious "WE" and clarify how you, as a family unit, are unique and have exciting things that you have faith in and do. When you share, permit your kids an opportunity to pose inquiries. You might need to think of some imaginary situations. These can be transformed into a game that allows your kids to rehearse the thoughts that you have examined.

Major issues.

It's additionally essential to convey that the necessities of the family override any one person. Making the daily practice of Family Nights all the time will enable every family part to have a spot to convey what needs be. This time for family holding joined with a place and time to be heard will assist everybody with getting tied up with the "WE" rather than the "Wii" idea. Moreover, make sure to convey those things which are entirely excluded. At the point when spoken about in highly contrasting terms, kids will comprehend and respect the limits significantly, and more regularly. For instance, smoking or physical brutality might be one of these significant issues. Be clear about the results of these behaviors and remember that while redundancy of the standards is substantial, be mindful so as not to concentrate on the negative always.

Do what needs to be done.

The best approach to truly make this work in your lives is to be sure that your day by day schedules mirror your beliefs. This is your Family Culture in real life. For example, if you accept that family time is significant, at that point, you may need to restrict every person's outside responsibilities, including yours! Family dinnertime is a considerable method to encourage family closeness, and it requires dedication on everybody's part. This is a case of a decision that you make that mirrors your needs. By reliably communicating this to your kids, you will find that they won't just get tied up with your Family Culture, however that they will keep you fair too.

Family Culture: Shared Identity and Belonging.

How would you hold a family together? How would you make kids WANT to invest energy with the family? How would you inspire your children to work things through with their kin and with you? A significant part of the appropriate response has to do with the family culture you make, which can take your family life from high to incredible. Here's the ticket.

1. Intentionally make a family personality.

You need this character to be specific and far-reaching, not restricting. Is yours an athletic family? Do all of you follow recent developments? Talk about who's understanding what? Most families have a few personalities: The Traveling Smiths can likewise be the Bookworm Smiths who love to cook together or gather amusing jokes.

2. Have supper together whenever possible.

Hint: It has nothing to do with the nourishment.

3. Hold onto any reason to celebrate and have a great time together.

Hold onto any reason to celebrate and have a ton of fun together whenever possible. Sock battles while collapsing clothing? Spontaneous sing-along melodies in the vehicle? A race to see who can take care of some groceries quickest? Food limericks at supper? Are they getting soaked in a warm summer downpour? The family that plays together forms a relationship that sticks together for the rough occasions. Also, they have a ton of fun!

4. Discover approaches to appreciate one another.

Her music decisions may sound like screaming you, and she may have no enthusiasm for that walk around the seashore that you need to feel alive. Be that as it may, if you put a little vitality into it, you will discover approaches to appreciate one another, regardless of whether it is cooking waffles together on Sunday morning or a shopping trip with lunch only for you two.

5. Respect each other's' interests.

Look into one another's interests. On the off chance that you began dating somebody whose principle enthusiasm was collectibles, you'd presumably need to comprehend what they adored about old things, and perhaps read a book or go with them on an antiquing attack. Your child's fixation on Star Wars books might appear to be an exercise in futility ("Why isn't he perusing the works of art?") yet your enthusiasm for catching wind of the plots, regardless of whether they all stable the equivalent from the start, will go far toward causing him to feel good talking with you about what's critical to him when something's disturbing him.

6. Keep the tone loving.

Each family unit has an emotional tone, which changes yet inclines toward a specific scope of notes. I tend towards a comfortable refuge feel, my better half leans toward interesting and rambunctious; either can be grasping. The fact of the matter is to see what makes dissonance and maintain a strategic distance from that. That may mean lessening screen time, or concurring that specific segments of the house are for calm interests, or just checking manners of speaking and reminding kids when they start yelling at one another. (Clearly, with little youngsters things will, in general, be noisy. However, that doesn't mean the tone isn't loving).

7. Grow family customs.

Customs, through their redundancy, fortify specific sentiments and qualities. They might be the absolute best apparatus in making family culture.

8. Consider drawing up a Family Mission articulation.

It might appear to be phony, yet families who do it say the procedure causes them to center around what makes a difference, and yearly audits/reworks keep them on track. There are numerous assets online to kick you off.

Necessary Steps to Build Your Family Culture.

What is family culture?

Family culture is an assortment of your family esteems, models and morals, and customs that your family clings to; a portion of these are passed down from ages to ages. Family culture is the thing that makes your family one of a kind as a unit. It is your personality; it is the thing that makes you known. On the off chance that you figure your family doesn't have a "personality," you are mixed up. Each family has this! Does your family talk before resting? Does your family like traveling? Does your family love music? Does your family like reading? Does your family appreciate expressions and artworks? Does your family have day by day or week after week family suppers? I am aware of families who completed school from a similar college or school, and they would go out to watch their school's games against their opponent groups. I am aware of families who consistently go on excursions each mid-year. I am aware of families who are continually joining fun runs.

For what reason is family culture significant?

Your family culture is significant because similar to your very own personality, and it's what makes your family your family. Family conflicts and difficulties uncover exactly how vital family culture is, as on account of kin competitions. At the point when family argues, it's not the recurrence nor the force of those arguments that characterize kin connections. Family culture and custom form little minutes that compensate for the troubles and conflicts. By building our own family culture, we can ensure our connection with our family. Family culture welcomes us to perceive how important the little things are. Through our family culture, we can return to something when our outer world turns out to be disproportionately demanding and excessively overpowering.

How would you fabricate your family culture?

Building your very own family culture is similarly as significant as discovering what it may be. Here are the means to assemble your very own family culture.

1. Recognize what your family culture.

It isn't so hard to recognize what your family culture is. You can begin by posting whatever appears to be part of your lifestyle all down in bullet points, or through a beautiful and fun activity called mind mapping. Mind mapping is an incredible instrument to uncover what different things we can partner to the focal thought. In discovering what your family culture is, you can put your family out and out in the focal point of it the guide, and from that point, attempt to offer "definitions" to your family. You can include simple essential words, values, or even exercises that you are as of now doing. What's more, you can make a different personality map for qualities or activities that you might want for your family to take a shot at.

Get a significant amount of paper, some bring markers, and start mind mapping! Before the finish of this action, you will have made a creepy-crawly like structure and thought of what your family's culture is.

2. Make it a habit.

In the wake of distinguishing the things that your family individuals partner to your family, you would now be able to start to continue doing it and transforming it into a habit.

3. Develop the significance of each a bith.

If something that your family values are adapting, at that point, a scrabble game night on Fridays could be something that you could do as an approach to strengthen the significance of this worth. We don't just stop at building these into routines. We constantly fortify these because there is an incentive to it. Having a family culture is significant because it gives you and your children the loving wellbeing net when things go troublesome. The thought behind making a family culture isn't to make a rundown of activities. It's tied in with discovering what your family trusts in, what your family values.

As your lives keep on pushing ahead, you will discover that a portion of your qualities or a part of the exercises that you have set up as a convention don't accommodate your way of life any longer. That is alright. There are a few exercises that you will develop out of; however, remember that the essential piece of these exercises you've manufactured is the inborn qualities that your family detracts from it. Your family culture is the thing that makes your family your own. Be glad for it and grasp it.

Approaches to Build a Healthy and Happy Family.

Since each family and every individual in it is one of a kind, there's no enchantment, one-size-fits-all parenting arrangement that is sure to give you a healthy and happy family. What's more, since nobody is immaculate in this fallen world, there's nothing of the sort as an ideal family. However, some essential rules will assist you with making a family in which every part can develop profoundly, emotionally, and socially - which will help you with building the healthy, happy family God needs you to appreciate.

Here's how you can make a healthy and happy family:
Be there. Your kids see your very nearness as an indication of minding and connectedness. You need to invest; however, much energy as could

reasonably be expected with them. Remember that your activity as a parent is a calling from God - more significant than some other work you do, including the event you get paid to do - and your impact on your kids will be your most prominent inheritance. Request that God assist you with making whatever penances you have to make to save your time and vitality to be there for your kids frequently. Be accessible to talk with them, help them, go to their occasions, and cheer them on in their different interests. Your kids ache for your essence, and nothing can compensate for your nonattendance. Be imaginative about how you can invest energy with every one of your kids one-on-one routinely, from going off a climb to playing a tabletop game together.

Express insistence, warmth, and encouragement. Parents who work on loving parenting, instead of disgrace-based parenting, will make a home where children and life partners have a sense of safety. So stay away from humiliation based parenting, which is execution arranged and endorsement centered, utilizing words and activities that cause kids to feel that they aren't cherished or essential. Instead, expect to create your kids to feel acknowledged, acknowledged, tuned in to, and entertained. Give your kids certainty by telling them that you have confidence in them, esteem them, and appreciate them. State "I love you" to them frequently, and give them a lot of physical warmth like embraces, kisses, and back rubs. As opposed to merely bouncing into their daily agendas with them, share some casual discussions with them after they return home from school, and before they head to sleep. Relinquish ridiculous desires for them. Encourage them to seek after their territories of intrigue and turn into the individuals God needs them to turn into.

Fabricate strong ethics and qualities. The choices that kids make today will regularly influence them for the remainder of their lives.

Concentrate the culture so you can comprehend what social impacts at present represent a danger to your kids. Petition God for God's assistance to encourage scriptural qualities and ethics to your kids in manners they can best learn. Talk transparently and genuinely with your kids about sex, liquor, and different medications from when they're youthful, entirely through their high schooler years, addressing their inquiries and examining issues in age-fitting ways. Encourage them to focus on carrying on with a way of life of immaculateness, incorporating regarding God with their bodies, reestablishing their psyches for good, turning their eyes and ears from what's useless, and guarding their hearts to the exclusion of everything else. Find a workable pace your kids watch on TV and in the motion pictures, what sites they visit, what music they tune in to, and what computer games they play. Watch and listen together with them as frequently as could be expected under the circumstances, and talk with them about the substance to assist them with figuring out how to contemplate it. Confine their entrance to offensive media content.

Discipline with consistency. At the point when you plainly express desires and reliably finish, you'll produce capable kids. Remember that steady control takes heaps of time and vitality. Request that God invigorate you, then you have to dedicate the vital time and energy as opposed to taking the path of least resistance when you are worn out and having your kids neglect to learn significant lessons. Recall God's guarantee that on the off chance that you train your kids in the manner they ought to go, when they're old, they won't withdraw from it. Set and impart healthy limits about doing schoolwork and tasks, coming clean, talking to you respectfully, and a bunch of different issues - and finish results when your kids settle on poor decisions. Help your kids choose what outcomes they ought to get for various infractions. Remain quiet - not angry - when you're teaching them, forgo annoying, pick your fights admirably, and show sympathy. Your readiness to be the parent they need - not merely a companion - will give them security and certainty.

Savagely wipe out the pressure. The uneven life won't be thoughtful to the regions you disregard. Request that God assist you with choosing which exercises to take out from your family's calendar in case you're too occupied even to consider getting enough rest and leisure time each day and night. Try not to disregard investing loads of energy with your family for anything, including your profession. Make whatever penances you have to make so you can appreciate a lot of loosened up family time together. Invest energy reflecting and imploring in isolation consistently to keep your life in the best possible point of view. Get enough rest and exercise regularly, and ensure that your partner and kids do, as well.

Impart well. Positive communication is the language of adoration for your kids. Make a propensity for listening cautiously to your kids at whatever point they share their contemplations and sentiments with you. Likewise, make sense of what different ways you can best express your adoration for your kids in manners that every one of them will get well. Apologize them to them when you've committed a parenting error. Permit the conflicts you experience with your life partner and kids to be a way to more profound communication by helping all of you see each other better and work as a group to tackle issues.

Play together. There is not at all like play to realize family harmony. Set aside a few minutes for excursions together, have a great time at home, go on visit trips (from getting frozen yogurt out to taking music or sports lessons together), share occasion conventions, appreciate humor together, and chip away at administration extends along. Sharing energetic experiences will fabricate family recollections that will bond all of you in incredible manners.

Love your companion. In case you're hitched, take a shot at your marriage regularly and put resources into it through exercises like incessant dates, since a loving marriage carries expectation and security to your kids. In case you're a single parent, assemble associations with others at your congregation who care about your kids and are happy to put resources into their lives.

Remember that the best things in life aren't things. Healthy stewardship and sound monetary choices produce definite family needs. Follow a spending limit to live underneath your methods, stay away from obligation, tithe and give in different liberal ways, and spare routinely. Displaying these healthy money-related practices will show your kids significant commonsense and profound lessons.

Invigorate your family's profound development. Your most prominent purpose in life is to leave an otherworldly heritage for your kids. So make your association with God through Christ your top need. Develop nearer to Christ exclusively and as a team with your life partner. Appeal to God for and with your kids in a standard family reverential time, compose a family constitution that depicts your family's qualities and talk about God frequently as you experience your regular exercises together.

Physiological Responses And Its Impact on Corporate and Family Culture.

The physiological factor is influencing people's character in a more significant number of ways than envisioned. Now and again, it is unpleasant and frightful. Now and again, it is a carousel and happy. Consequently, life is being influenced by the blended sentiment of dread, stress, strain, joy, and satisfaction. This period of human beings that doesn't get enacted in a dynamic mode in adulthood alone. These emotions and manifestations stayed dormant in childhood, and consider the situational premise in adulthood. It decreases in mature age, leaving numerous elderly individuals to degrade. What elements are administering this specific stage in people involves extraordinary worry to all?

The physiological impact can be seen thoroughly if we assess and dissect the essential socio-mental idea and psychophysiology. The summary of the continuing point is clarified in the accompanying passage. Psychophysiology is firmly identified with the field of Neuroscience and Social neuroscience, which frets about connections between mental occasions and brain reactions. Psychophysiology is likewise identified with the restorative discipline known as psychosomatics.

We would now be able to assess how profound and practical the bond between psychophysiology and brain reactions. The brain reactions do influence day by day life of individuals, in one way or the other. They are testing further; the effect of responses in human character required careful investigation as opposed to getting hasty. There are numerous perspectives and modalities influencing people. Nonetheless, I am focusing on "corporate managers" contribution to their business culture.

The "corporate managers" job is requesting the gainfulness and smooth working of the business. The duties and weight of work do influence their private life and their families. The desires are strong, and activity should have been active and proficient. It requires a change in outlook in their official and individual dealings. It is an essential part of their expert and residential capacities requiring adjusting the way to deal with it that meets both the closures.

The connection among managers and their partners, the two seniors and youngsters require a subjective methodology and durable power for smooth working. This duty lies similarly among all individuals from an association. An inquiry emerges, regardless of whether an intellectual style is submitted or passive? An investigation proposed that intuitive pioneers might not be so much commanding but rather more sustaining than their expository associates and that they are more enjoyed and respected by scientific individuals than diagnostic pioneers are by instinctive individuals.

It is, in this manner, critical for the corporate chief and top managerial staff to be increasingly adaptable and versatile in their methodology. It causes them to sift through the distinctions among managers and laborers. The complaint and contrast of conclusions among every individual from an association ought to be confined inside the parameters of the organization's advantage alone. Any deviation ought not to be encouraged; else, it will boomerang with equivalent power.

The managers ought to and must isolate their day by day schedule in such a way, that their authority and family life is reasonably advocated. He ought not to worry about the concern of family gives influencing his corporate intrigue either straightforwardly or by implication.

Here, the family ties assume a significant job making his corporate culture a reasonable power to deal with. The healthy local climate will effectively and professionally change his expert methodology. It will show the development and smooth working of the organization. Also, it is making family life a attractive and happy substance.

CHAPTER NINE

HOW TO ENCOURAGE A HAPPY ENVIRONMENT.

Bringing up Happy Children.

It is the unavoidable truth that children can adapt better in a circumstance where there are no stresses and differences. There is another fact of life that bringing up happy children who need more consideration and care. It is exceptionally troublesome on the off chance that you don't set a few standards to follow. Everybody wants happiness for their children more than all else, and it is the fundamental wish of any parents; in this way, they make a decent attempt to satisfy every one of the desires and needs of their children to fulfill them. The quest for satisfaction never ends.

There are some fundamental tips on how to bring up happy children; one of the essential things which you should tell your children is that the amount that you love them and the amount you care for them. Attempt to show your adoration with its full importance, for example, embrace them, and kiss them so they can understand that their parents love them. On the off chance that you show your affection towards your children, this expands their certainty level just as it fabricates a constructive character. Another significant issue that will help you in bringing up happy children is consistently attempting to tune in to your child mindfully, and this gives them safety that they are significant. You are keen on listening to what they need to state. Pay attention to them and consistently give them some additional opportunity to tune in.

The most significant thing, which influences the character of your children most is the climate of the home, where they invest a ton of energy. If the environment of the house isn't happy and liberated from all threatening impedance, at that point, the character of the child won't grow appropriately. Also, on the off chance that you give them a pleasant and cordial climate, their nature and inward capacities come to bleeding edge all the more unmistakably. They will take things all the more decidedly, and their methodology towards them will be clear.

Attempt to develop the certainty of your child; this is possible if you value the work that he accomplished for you. Tell your child that you need his assistance since this is an excellent approach to get his help, attempt to encourage them. Try not to unsettle him by demoralizing and discovering problems in his work. Be that as it may, at some point, his assistance can expand your job; however, don't attempt to discourage him. Since these things build up the awareness of other's expectations in the child and the child, he believes that he can support his parents. Continuously attempt to commend their great work just as make the alteration when there is a need. At the point when you try to state something on his mix-up and definitely don't say he isn't right, you need to ask him for what good reason the behavior isn't proper and improper.

Communicating With Children and Family.

Communicating with our children and family is tied in with relating in adoration, one on one, with every individual from that family. From one point of view, we don't pick our family from inception. From a higher point of view, we do. We choose our parents and our family; we select the individuals who will assist us with building up our character and qualities, and we do as such for the test such education will offer us in our life journey. Similarly, as we have picked, at a spirit level, our parents and family, so have our children! We, as parents, may well accept this open the door to ensure we offer the best qualities and life openings we can for our children. We can begin by opening wide the lines of communication with our children and family individuals.

How would we open wide these lines of communication? Think about how you like to feel when somebody speaks with you, verbally or in other increasingly subtle ways. How would you want others to treat you or approach you when they need to talk? You want to feel the other individual respects you and your thoughts and that they love you similarly, right? You want to feel respected and adored. Thus does everybody, particularly your partner, children, and other family individuals.

So communication inside the family is tied in with interfacing at a fundamentally close to home level. We are communicating what? Anything you desire, however, vested continuously in love. Love in the entirety of its horde angles. Love acknowledges a decent variety and cheers in contrast. Ordinarily, in the family structure, we as of now share such a lot, and one of the greatest delights of the family is celebrating our similarities, yet additionally, our differences. Formed in a similar soil of the emotional and physical ties we share, having a place with family offers our essential and early personality.

So when we identify with our children, in their family of the cause, which we, as parents, are planning for them, our obligation to adore and acknowledge every child similarly as they seem to be, is of foremost significance. These little ones, spotless, typically, and understanding, have the right to experience childhood in an environment where they can don't hesitate to express their creative mind in any capacity they want. Allow them to sing and act and run and talk and convey what needs to be freed from approved limitations and critical limits.

Children need direction and look for courses, acknowledgment, and encouragement from their parents. Capable love that aides and educates are an incredible blessing we offer our children. They seek us for authority and endorsement. The endorsement is another name for loving acknowledgment and upbeat encouragement to turn out to be more and to build up their very own one of a kind individual character and qualities. It is our benefit as parents to offer this degree of security and love to our children.

We can invest quality energy with our children, teaching by loving model admirably well, and doing fun exercises altogether. In your communications, ensure nothing is forbidden. Children need to don't hesitate to talk about anything with their parents, straightforwardly, and sure they will be heard and acknowledged.

Children, similarly as we do ourselves, love to feel some portion of a one of a kind and different group: family. This feeling of having a place is essential with a child's perception of individual worth and significant commitment. As our children perceive how we love and respect them unequivocally, they will figure out how to do likewise. They will learn resistance, acknowledgment of contrast, transparency, self-articulation, or more all, adoration. Ideally, they will, in later life, have numerous superb and happy recollections of experiencing childhood in the family we have housed them.

Eating With Children.

All children experience eating stages - some eat almost no portions while others eat exceptionally restricted portions. In any case, you genuinely don't need to stress; as long as they are eating something and have enough vitality for their exercises, they are excellent. Exacting eaters are an unadventurous part who can drive any parent over the edge with their consistent difference in preferences. They may, for instance, decide to eat just fish pieces for quite a long time and afterward unexpectedly conclude that they've become wary of them. At that point, there is the Beige Food Eater, who, as the name proposes, eats just beige or white foods.

The primary worry for parents is whether their child is getting enough sustenance. Pediatricians will console that as long as the child is on the development bend, has enough vitality, and is happy, and there is not a lot to stress over. Young children (9 months to 3 years of age) lose enthusiasm for eating since they are too busy with investigating their tremendous world, so they depend on juices and milk to top off their bellies before hustling off to the opposite side of the room or peering out the window to watch traffic. During childhood, being exacting towards nourishment isn't a dietary issue; however, merely part of growing up. It's a stage they will exceed in the long run. Meanwhile, parents can make a healthy and empowering environment for their meticulous eaters:

· Do a self-assessment by inquiring as to whether you are a picky eater as well? Children are incredibly equipped for watching and impersonating their parents, so observe how you act during dinner times to encourage inspirational frames of mind at the eating table.

· Limit the admission of snacks before dinnertime.

· On the off chance that your child doesn't eat vegetables, get the necessary supplements from organic products or different nourishments.

· Offer littler segments each opportunity to restrict left-overs.

· Facilitate the nerves of "eating enough" through encouragement. "That is incredible! Do you want more?" works superior to "Gracious dear! Why aren't you eating anything?"

· Abstain from making influences or giving prizes. This just guarantees momentary accomplishment with confounding effects. For instance, when you reveal to them, they will get dessert if they finish the entirety of their vegetables, the estimation of the plants will diminish because of their expanded enthusiasm for the frozen yogurt. Despite everything, they won't make the most of their vegetables over the long haul.

Picky eaters are delicate towards what they eat. They, for the most part, aren't testing you, so don't transform this into a force battle. Let your child comprehend that he needs to deal with his body, and he needs various kinds of foods to be healthy. Let him take an interest in arranging supper with the goal that he feels less confined. Recall the brilliant standard: dinners should be appreciated, not constrained. Try not to surrender! Continue acquainting new foods with your child. When recognizable, he may be happy to try them. At the point when your child feels hungry, he will eat. This is an endurance test that he gets it. Maybe without the pressure, he will welcome the eating experience more. On the off chance that you are still stressed, visit a pediatrician for more appeal.

Raising Confident, Curious and Creative Kids.

What do you wish the most for your kids? Is it an existence of satisfaction where they appreciate every minute by thinking about their life as an experience? Or on the other hand, is it an actual existence where they can carry on with their life courageously by using intuition inventively in their day by day life? Whatever be the fantasies we have for our kids, creative mind, inventiveness, interest, and trust in children do assume a significant job in understanding these fantasies. It is, without a doubt, conceivable to bring up our kids to be inventive, challenging, and confident on the off chance that we parents have the fundamental comprehension and information to journey their imagination. On top, it isn't such a hard procedure.

Asking why? Because kids are brought into the world interested. That we should encourage them in their exploratory undertakings, children have a natural quality to retain data effectively; thus, when we develop their feeling of experience, it will rouse the kids to make a special effort in learning and seeing new things. The more things they find for themselves, the more effective it is for them to think of imaginative thoughts. In all honesty, all these are not simple on paper, yet additionally as a general rule as they are a few straightforward things that we can do to encourage their interest.

Imaginative reasoning is significant for children as it creates personal inspiration in children. This encourages them to adore the way toward learning for an incredible duration. Also, interest and imagination are identified with ideal prosperity as it is observed that the individuals who love adapting new things and are always curious are more happy and idealistic than the individuals who are most certainly not. This gives them a feeling of self-certainty that makes them propel themselves more to follow their dreams, regardless of the substantial number of obstacles that they face throughout everyday life. Don't we as a whole need our children to pursue their hopes and dreams?

For this to occur, the main thing required is for the parents to be prepared. Parents impact what their child thinks and learns in the early years. Parents are the excellent primary examples that the kids turn to. Parents should help them in showing the kids to see how to think, yet then never show them what to believe as it will prevent their imagination and interest.

Presently, it is the ideal opportunity for the tips which will assist us with raising sure, curious, and inventive kids. A portion of these are:

1. Encouraging Curiosity.

Asking inquiries to children is an extraordinary method to upgrade their interest. It won't be uneven, as you previously speculated, since it is typical information that kids are specialists in asking questions. This two-way process is indeed an unusual and least demanding approach to support their interest. It spurs the kids to discover answers for themselves and advances their autonomy, continuously attempting to extend their insight.

2. Communication.

Communicate with the kids those issues, which will make them think. This gives them a possibility or capacity to manufacture their very own sentiments. At the point when this sort of communication occurs, you will ready to assist their interest just as you increase their certainty. Children become increasingly attentive and discerning about their environment. Also, it causes the parents to comprehend what every one of the kids is genuinely keen on.

3. Open Atmosphere.

This is a basic essential since the kids can express the thoughts completely just in such an environment where there isn't a lot of restraints. At the point when children search out new trials and new ideas, they can build their underlying reasoning and their capacity to tackle issues.

4. Adequate Resources.

When we give sufficient assets to unstructured and unlimited child coordinated exercises in the right direction, we are giving them enough space to abundant development of imaginative articulations. It isn't hard since we can utilize our very own regular experiences as opposed to purchasing costly and extravagant materials.

5. Building Confidence.

If we truly need our kids to be satisfied, then the kids ought to be made to take a look at things in other points of view and ways and afterward cause the kids to trust in them by putting stock in them. This like this would assist with supporting the child's advantages.

6. Allowing Mistakes.

It is particularly conceivable that there would be bunches of errors in this intriguing procedure. The significant thing to note here is that the missteps made by the kids ought to be considered as circumstances and not as fruitless endeavors. Just when we enable the kids to commit errors, will they not fear disappointments. On the off chance that the kids are frightened of frustrations; at that point, there is a lesser possibility of them attempting new things.

7. Timely Appreciation.

Show and exhibit certified intrigue and energy about what they are doing - Most of the time, the kids can comprehend when we fake these emotions. Be with them when you have the opportunity since that excites the children most.

Through these ways, we will have the option to shape an environment for the kids where they are loaded with interest and be brimming with trust in both themselves and their general surroundings. Parents likewise wish that their kids are confident, curious, and inventive! So here come, some essential hints that empower us to do that!

Step by step instructions to impart pastimes to kids.

One of the least demanding and most significant approaches to construct a child's self-esteem is to invest energy with them accomplishing something that they appreciate, as well as value. There is an exceptional enchantment that occurs between a parent and a child when they share a commonly adored moment. It sends the message to the child that their parents are having a ton of fun, genuine, legitimate, real enjoyment with them! There is nothing all the more approving for a child to see their parent having a good time while investing energy with them. It sets a solid establishment for extraordinary self-esteem and certainty that their essence and friends aren't just valued; however, delighted in and that they are deserving of others' consideration, warmth, and time. Every single beneficial thing!

Not exclusively does a distinct intrigue advantage a child's self-esteem, it is additionally an incredible holding opportunity. Kids learn, convey, and feel great through play. Even though both of the exercises highlighted in the recordings are melodic, despite everything, we'll think of it as a play because, for kids, it fills a similar need. Playing with your child sets up the trust and a guarantee (maybe) that you can convey and comprehend them on their level, which may make them increasingly slanted to impart things to you through play or even outside of play, realizing that you are "with them".

Offering a premium and playing to your child likewise sets such a significant case of teaching your child that it's alright to discover some new information (and not be an ace from the beginning). For instance, perhaps you're evaluating another tune or learning another harmony, odds are you won't get it directly on the initial attempt, and this is such a decent method to show kids that it's alright. It's ordinary, and it's a significant piece of learning and life. Possibly you took in another tune, and you've played it a bundle, yet despite everything you mess up one harmony part of the way through and hello, what another great message, botches occur, we're human, and we state "oh no" and attempt once more. Once more, kids learn through play and display, and the models are parents set. What preferable path over to accomplish something enjoyment with your child that you will both appreciate.

It's a well-known fact that I love games. I have a computer game reassure guided into all of our TVs. My storm cellar has boxes and boxes loaded with tabletop games. I have a 20-sided kick the bucket inked on my body. Games (computer games, table games, pretending games) are something I do a great deal. However, when my kids request to play, it very well may be challenging to suit them. Sharing my side interests — games just as baseball, drawing, motion pictures, and different things — can be challenging to do with kids so young. In any case, they're into whatever their father is into — despite everything they believe, and I'm cool! — So I need to engage them however much as could reasonably be expected. I've put forth a valiant effort to give them access to my universes a smidgen, and I've found a couple of things you may likewise discover effective.

Let them go along with you. Little ones need to spend time with mother and father now and again. Let them participate in the good times. That may mean downshifting from "Mass Effect" to a session of "Furious Birds," however they'll be so thankful they could mess around with you.

Try not to constrain it. The most exceedingly terrible thing you can do is attempt to restrict your side interests on their kids. How frequently have we seen a hopeless child being hauled to baseball training while father believes it's the best thing ever? Or, on the other hand, a parent compelling some exemplary band on a child who needs to hear Taylor Swift? Push it on them, and they'll despise it. Let them appreciate it in their particular manner, and they'll, you know, appreciate it.

Discover something suitable that you additionally appreciate. I can't play brutal computer games — "Obligation at hand," "Inhabitant Evil," "Mortal Kombat" — around my kids. I likewise don't feel right listening to certain music — any pop melody with savagery or sex — around them either. "Alright, for kids" doesn't generally liken to "childish". You can discover something you dig out that is OK for them to expend.

Now and then, you can fake it. My kids regularly intrude on me reading a book or playing a computer game. They need me to reveal to them the story. They need to play the game. I've been known to condense a book I'm perusing in kid-accommodating terms or hand over a controller that is not in any case connected. They appreciate the minute and move onto the following thing.

Present your interest in their terms. My child adores baseball. Indeed, he says he does. I think he just prefers to sit on the sofa with me. He asks what they're doing. I could go on throughout the day about the Mets and the better standards of baseball, yet he'll quit listening before

133

long. What works better: "That person tosses the ball, and the other person attempts to hit it". Simple.

Look into what they're doing. As opposed to attempting to twist your side interests into a child open course, join your kids in what they're doing. Play computer games they like. Read the books they need. Draw superheroes with them. They'll cherish the time you go through with them.

CHAPTER TEN

HAPPY SIBLINGS; CREATE A CONNECTION WITH EACH ONE OF YOUR CHILDREN.

Need to be an incredible parent? Need to raise a happy, healthy, respectful child? Need to live in a home where discipline gets unnecessary? The mystery is to take a closer association with your child. It isn't sufficient that we tell our children we love them. We have to place our adoration without hesitation consistently for them to feel it.

"In any case, I don't get that's meaning, placing our affection without hesitation?"

For the most part, it implies making that association with our child our most noteworthy need. Love in real life involves giving keen consideration to what goes on between us, seeing things from our child's perspective, and continually remembering that this child who at times may make us insane is as yet that valuable infant we invited into our arms with such expectation.

"Doesn't that make a ton of energy?"

It requires a great deal of exertion to take care of another individual completely, however when we are truly present with our child, and we regularly find that it stimulates us and causes us to feel progressively alive, as being utterly current with anybody does. Being near another human takes work. However, 90% of individuals on their deathbed state that their greatest lament is that they didn't draw nearer to the individuals in their lives. What's more, practically all parents whose children are grown state they wish they had invested more energy with their kids.

"Being completely present? How might I do that when I'm simply attempting to eat on the table and prevent from stumbling over the toys?"

Being available just methods focusing. Like a marriage or a kinship, your association with your child needs positive regard for growth. Consideration = Love. Like your nursery, your vehicle, or your work, what you take care of twists. What's more, that sort of mindfulness requires some serious energy. You can perform multiple tasks at it while you're making supper, yet the mystery of an incredible relationship is some engaged time each day going to just to that child.

"This is very ambiguous for me. What am I expected to DO?"

1. Start directly for a firm establishment.

The closeness of the parent-child association all through life results from how a lot of parents interface with their children directly from the earliest starting point. For example, look into has demonstrated that fathers who take possibly more than seven days off work when their infants are conceived have a closer association with their child

136

at each stage, including as adolescents and understudies. Are these circumstances and logical results? The scholars state that if a man bonds with his infant, he will remain nearer to her all through life. Yet, you don't need to accept that holding with an infant is vital to take note of that the sort of man who cherishes his infant and supports his new family is probably going to keep doing as such in manners that bring them closer all through her childhood.

2. Remember that all connections take work.

Significant parent-child associations don't spring all of a sudden, anything else than great marriages does. Science gives us a head start - on the off chance that we weren't organically customized to cherish our newborn children humanity would have ceased to exist quite a while in the past - yet as kids get more seasoned, we have to expand on that common bond, or the difficulties of present-day life can dissolve it. Fortunately, children naturally love their parents. For whatever length of time that we don't blow that, we can keep the association reliable.

3. Organize time with your child.

Accept that you'll have to place in a lot of time making a decent association with your child. Quality time is a fantasy because there's no change to turn on closeness. Envision that you work regularly, and have put aside a night with your significant other, whom you've scarcely found in the previous a half year. Does he promptly begin opening up about his inner feelings? Not likely.

Just being around someone, without amount, doesn't equal quality. You can't expect a decent association with your girl if you invest all your energy at work, and she invests all her time with her companions. So as hard for what it's worth with the weights of employment and day by day life, if we need a superior relationship with our kids, we need to save an opportunity to get that going.

4. Start with trust, the establishment of each great relationship.

Trust starts in the early stages when your child realizes whether she can rely upon you to get her when she needs you. When infants are a year old, scientists can survey whether children are "safely joined" to their parents, which fundamentally implies the infant believes that his parents can be relied upon to meet his emotional and physical needs. After some time, we procure our children's trust in different manners: finishing on the guarantee we make to play a game with them later, not breaking a certainty, getting them on schedule.

Simultaneously, we stretch out our trust to them by anticipating the best from them and having confidence in their central goodness and potential. We trust in the intensity of human improvement to enable our child to develop, learn, and develop. We believe that even though our child may act like a child today, the individual in question is continually forming into a progressively full-grown individual (similarly as, ideally, we will be). We believe that regardless of what the person in question does, there is consistently the potential for constructive change.

Trust doesn't mean aimlessly accepting what your teenager lets you know. Trust implies not abandoning your child, regardless of what the person does. Trust involves failing to walk away from the relationship in disappointment since you believe that she needs you and that you will figure out how to function things out.

5. Encourage, Encourage, Encourage.

Think about your child as a plant that is modified naturally to develop and bloom. On the off chance that you see the plant has darker leaves, you consider if possibly it needs increasingly light, more water, more manure. You don't criticize it and yell at it to fix itself and develop right.

Kids structure their perspective on themselves and the world consistently. They need your encouragement to consider themselves to be acceptable individuals who can do beneficial things. What's more, they have to know you're their ally. If the majority of what leaves your mouth is recompense or analysis, they won't like themselves, and they won't feel like you're their partner. You lose your solitary leverage with them, and they fail something each child needs: to realize they have a grown-up who respects them.

6. Recall that respect must be familiar.

Entirely self-evident, isn't that so? In any case, we overlook this with our kids, since we realize we should be the chief. You can even now set points of confinement (and you should), however on the off chance that you do it respectfully and with compassion, your child will learn both to approach others with respect and to hope to be dealt with courteously himself.

When I got agitated with my then multi-year old, he went to me and said: "I don't care for it when you talk to me that way". A companion who was with us stated, "If he's beginning this early, you will have large issues when he's a teenager!" Actually, instead of testing my position, my toddler was essentially requesting to be treated with the nobility he had generally expected. Presently a teenager, he keeps on treating himself, me, and others respectfully. Also, he picks peers who treat him respectfully. Isn't that what we as a whole need for our kids?

7. Consider connections the moderate growth of every day cooperations.

You don't need to do anything exceptional to manufacture an relationship with your child. The great - and awful - news is that each cooperation makes the relationship. Shopping for food, carpooling, and shower time matter as much as that grandiose talk you have when there's an issue. He wouldn't like to share his toy, or hit the sack, or get his work done? How you handle it is one step in the establishment of your lasting relationship, just as his thoughts regarding all connections.

That is one explanation that merits thoroughly considering any repetitive cooperations that drive you up the wall to perceive how you may unexpectedly deal with them. Cooperations that happen more than once will, in general, start an example. Pestering and reprimanding is no reason for an association with somebody you love. What's more, your life is too unreasonably short for you to spend it in a condition of irritation.

8. Communication propensities start early.

Do you listen when she drives on endlessly about her companions at preschool, in any event, when you have progressively essential things to consider? At that point, she's bound to inform you regarding her connections with young men when she's fourteen. It's difficult to focus when you're hurrying to get nourishment for supper and return home, yet if you aren't generally listening, two things occur. You ruin a chance to find out about and show your child, and she discovers that you don't regularly tune in, so there's the minimal point in talking.

9. Try not to think about it literally.

Your teenager hammers the entryway to her room. Your teenager spats, "Mother, you never listen!" Your teenager shouts, "I hate you, Daddy!" What's the most significant thing to recall? Try not to think about it literally! This isn't basically about you, and it's about them: their tangled up sentiments, their trouble controlling themselves, their juvenile capacity to comprehend, and express their feelings. Thinking about it wounds you, which implies you do what we as a whole do when harmed: either close off, or lash out, or both, which compounds a predicament for all concerned.

Recalling not to think about if it implies you:

- Take a full breath.

- Let the hurt go.

- Remind yourself that your child does, in reality, love you yet can't connect with it right now.

- Consciously speak with a softer tone.

- Try challenging to recollect what it feels like to be a child who is vexed and over-responding.

- Think through how to react tranquility and productively.

You can even now set breaking points, yet you do it from as quiet a spot as you can summon. Your child will be profoundly appreciative, regardless of whether she can't recognize it right now. I'm not for a moment proposing that you let your child treat you disrespectfully. I'm suggesting you carry on of affection, as opposed to anger, as you set points of confinement. What's more, in case you're too furious even to consider getting in contact with your affection right now, at that point pause.

10. Oppose the drive to be right.

How might you feel about somebody who hurt, undermined, or mortified you, "to your benefit"? Kids do require our direction, yet rebuffing your child consistently dissolves your relationship, which causes your child to get out of hand more. See Positive Discipline for more data on taking care of your anger and setting useful points of confinement.

11. Try not to let little breaks develop.

On the off chance that something's incorrectly between you, figure out how to bring it up and work it through entirely. Deciding to pull back (except briefly, deliberately) when your child appears to be determined to pushing you away is ALWAYS a slip-up. Each trouble is a chance to draw nearer or make the separation.

12. Re-interface after each separation.

Parents usually give a handle, or compass, for kids to join to and remain situated around. At the point when they're separated from us, they need a substitute, so they locate themselves around instructors, mentors, hardware, or friends. At the point when we rejoin each other physically, we have likewise to rejoin emotionally.

13. Remain accessible.

Most kids don't keep an agenda and bring things up at a booked gathering. What's more, nothing makes them quiet down quicker than squeezing them to talk. Kids talk when something is up for them, especially if you've demonstrated yourself to be a decent audience, however not excessively joined to their opening up to you.

Being available when they return home is an excellent approach to hear the features of the day with more youthful kids, and even, frequently, with more seasoned ones. With more established kids, just being in a similar room, accomplishing something can make the open door for connection. In case you're preparing supper, and she's doing schoolwork, for example, or you two are in the vehicle alone, there's regularly an opening. If one of you is slouched over the PC, the collaboration is probably going to be progressively restricted. See ways as in vicinity where you're both possibly accessible, without it appearing to be an interest.

This may appear glaringly evident, yet expressing your accessibility is useful, even with teenagers. Be that as it may, the most significant piece of remaining accessible is a perspective. Your child will detect your emotional accessibility. Parents who have intimate associations with their youngsters regularly state that as their child has gotten more established, they've made it a training to drop everything else if their adolescent signals a longing to talk. This can be troublesome in case you're likewise taking care of a requesting work and different

143

obligations. However, kids who feel that different things are increasingly imperative to their parents regularly look somewhere else when they're emotionally penniless. What's more, that is our misfortune, as much as theirs.

Effective Ways Communication With Your Child.

Since humanity's commencement, communication has assumed a crucial job in creating withstanding connections among people. Without language and non-verbal methods for conveying everything that needs to be sent, we wouldn't have the option to pass data and even help other people. In any case, the relationship set up between individuals from a similar family has never been so affected by the quick-paced life that we are on the whole living today. Taking everything into account, parents endeavor these days, presumably over a couple of decades prior, to keep alive conventional qualities like an effective two route communication with their children.

Two routes for this situation implies bidirectional. It is the necessary information that it takes two, the producer and the recipient, and an agreeable, active channel, to impart. On the off chance that anything, educational hypothesis shows us as parents that the earlier we implement positive examples of communications, the higher are the odds that our children will learn and apply them later on. There are likewise other colossally advantageous results in having a robust association with your child:

- As a parent, your input, guidance, encouragement, and examination prompts healthy self-esteem and self-certainty for your child. Denouncing, evaluate, and accuse will have inverse impacts.

- Respecting your child's emotions or perspective and attempting to comprehend them will reduce the odds of insubordination and misbehavior when children grow up.

- Building a positive and robust method for communication with your child from the beginning guarantees a longstanding and productive relationship that you will both appreciate as you become more seasoned.

- To arrive at the objective of having a fruitful two route communication with your child, parents don't need to do the incomprehensible, but instead littler, more natural things like:

- When your child looks grieved, meditative, or is exceptionally quiet, you have to quit collapsing the naturally washed garments, prevent from hacking the carrots or from staring at the TV, etc., and focus on your child's body language. Start from that point. Encourage him/her to talk about what is on his/her brain straightforwardly. Ensure that your voice is delicate to make a close and safe setting, indicating both comprehension and backing for anything he/she needs to state.

- When your child is excited about something and truly needs to impart that to you, once more, drop all that you are doing and listen persistently. It is fundamental to show children that nothing is a higher priority than what they need to state.

Additionally, they will discover that listening is a piece of communication procedure.

- Remember to adjust your jargon to words that your children can comprehend and be predictable in your behavior towards them. If you need your message to break through to them, you need to draw their consideration, clarify just as conceivable what you mean, and afterward rehash yourself to ensure they get you.

Speak With Toddlers, Laying the Foundation For When They Are Teenagers.

What an overwhelming assignment, the magnificent duty of raising toddlers. As a married parent of six children and all genuinely close in age we were continually told by individuals "Gracious, how are you going to manage when they are teenagers" and my response to them was, we have enough to manage now, we'll cross that bridge when we come to it. Much to my dismay that, what we do while they are youthful toddlers, lays such a solid establishment for the remainder of their lives and the environment we make as parents for these little youngsters, will at last build up my capacity to speak with them when they are teenagers.

I can't emphasize enough the significance of being parents that are both in agreement! We have to speak with one another, ensuring that the environment stays a steady one. Talk about with one another the limits that you will both set and how you need to bring your children up, obviously if you are a solitary parent, and this won't generally be an issue. We can't give our children blended messages as they will rapidly pick on that and figure out how to skilfully play on it. At the point when you, as their Mum disapproves of something your child needs, then the Dad needs likewise to say no, or in like manner, Mum needs to help Dad, without the contrast of failing or faltering. The child will discover that you are both associated with their prosperity and will develop to respect that.

Communicating with your toddlers on their level is an essential key to progress. Giving guidance or clarifications to their inquiries that they don't comprehend will only motivate them to inquire as to why. We have to abstain from utilizing articulations like "since I said" This won't generally fulfill their interest. In any case, be conclusive and direct with our answers, talking with a friendly tone, recollecting that there is something else entirely to communication than merely the words we express. Ensure that you are exceptionally cautious about what body language and outward appearance you are utilizing, kids will pick up on this, and it is similarly as significant as what you say.

By communicating with our child appropriately and being joined as parents are presumably one of the most important keys to raising toddlers. It just outcomes in them talking about significant issues with us as they grow up.

Speak With Your Teenagers Effectively.

It is difficult to recall that you were at one time a teenager yourself. The fights with your parents over your privileges and requirements put upon you. Presently you are a parent to teenage children, and recollections of your high schooler years are long gone. You see, your sweet, lovable kids currently grown up into touchy and contentious teenagers who stay secured up their rooms and are progressively adapt to focus on the music blasting through their earphones than anything you need to state.

The enticement is there to let them would what they like to stay away from the frightful fights; however, it doesn't generally need to end in a significant battle. In all honesty, there is an approach to talk with them and develop a relationship by and by.

On the off chance that the line of communication has been set up with your kids since early on, then proceeding through their teenage years is much less testing. As far back as my children began school, I would ask them how their day in school went, who their companions were, and what they realized at school. Sooner or later, they became acclimated to having this discussion and would get back home from school and reveal to me insights regarding their day without me in any event, asking them any longer. Children become accustomed to schedules, and once the everyday practice of discussions with their parents have been built up, they are increasingly inclined to join it into their day by day schedule.

You know your children well and will see that something isn't exactly right when they would prefer not to talk about their day, or they exclude talking about their closest friend. Without the standard daily schedule of discussion, you could always be unable to identify that something isn't directly as there would be nothing to analyze. This is an ideal opportunity to address them and inquire as to whether everything worked out in a right way and disclosed to them why you are asking, for example on the off chance that they dither to talk about their ongoing math test, at that point you should scrutinize your child concerning how they figure they did on the math test. When they realize you are enlightened, they will open up and give you the subtleties.

My very own little girl got so used to disclosing to me about her friends, her rivals, and even sweethearts that I am the first individual she calls to talk to about anything significant going on in her life. She comes to me for advice on managing circumstances throughout her life and trusts in me before any of her girlfriends. It is stunning how this sort of communication can assemble such a stable connection among parent and child. After some time, my little girl experienced her dearest friends double-crossing her, and when she disclosed to me that I was the main that is consistently there for her, I realized I had accomplished something right.

Keep on asking your children questions about their lives and find a workable pace buddy. It is continuously a smart thought to have them welcome their friends over to your home, not exclusively will you find a good pace they are spending time with however you can breathe easy because of realizing they are sheltered at home as opposed to meandering the streets someplace or hanging out in foundations that may not generally have the best notoriety.

They are a companion just as a parent goes far in holding with your teenagers. Attempting to discover the harmony between both is a precious instrument with regards to effective parenting. Remember that your kids will address their companions, and on the off chance that you can figure out how to be a companion just as a parent, they will feel increasingly useful in communicating with you on this level.

Printed in Great Britain
by Amazon

49600553R00088